Praise for
THE NARROW PATH

"In *The Narrow Path*, Rich unpacks what living our best life truly looks like. By challenging some of our most basic assumptions about what it is to walk with Jesus and by inviting us to discover whether we are on the broad or narrow path, Rich inspires us to get on the right path so we can live the abundant life Jesus came to give us. This book is a much-needed heart checkup for every Jesus follower."
—CHRISTINE CAINE, founder of A21 and Propel Women

"A book written for all those 'who are weary of anchoring their lives in the unfulfilling promises of the surrounding culture,' those who find the broad way, essentially, 'do whatever you want and follow the crowd,' to be revealing itself as exactly what Jesus warned—a path toward death, not life—and those who are interested, intrigued, and deeply drawn to the possibility of Jesus and his narrow way."
—JOHN MARK COMER, author and founder of Practicing the Way

"If you're tired of the choice between a half-Christian, conscience-quieting religion and an exhausting, guilt-inducing moralism, this book is for you. With a map through Jesus's Sermon on the Mount, Rich Villodas leads us to the narrow path and shows us how to find joy on that road. You won't regret the trip!"

—Russell Moore, editor-in-chief of *Christianity Today*

"Rich Villodas is one of the necessary voices of our time. As we wrestle to understand how Jesus speaks to our current day, Rich makes the words of Christ accessible. Leaders like him are rare. This book is needed."

—Lecrae, Grammy Award–winning artist and producer

"We live in a world that hollows us into flimsy, frightened shadows of what God intends for us to be. Into this wasteland comes Rich Villodas, a pastor full of conviction and hope, a man who knows not only how to talk about his subject matter but also how to walk in it. Brilliant and beautiful, concise and clear, *The Narrow Path* helps us remember again the words of our Lord that lead us to the liberating reality of a world in which less is more, in which the hard work of obedience leads to durable joy, and in which the love of Jesus is to be discovered and dwelt in while we travel this road together as a body of fellow pilgrims."

—Curt Thompson, MD, psychiatrist and author of *The Deepest Place* and *The Soul of Shame*

"This is Rich Villodas at his pastoral best. His writing shimmers with grace, reflecting the radiance of a kingdom vision of the good life. It is obvious that the words of Jesus's most significant sermon have passed through the depths of Rich's own heart. They emerge through his stories and scars to meet us in the realities of our world. Challenging and confronting, these are pastoral reflections for everyone, calling us to the narrow path toward an expansive life."

—GLENN PACKIAM, lead pastor of Rockharbor Church and author of *The Resilient Pastor* and *The Intentional Year*

"By bringing laser focus to the manifesto of our faith—the Sermon on the Mount—Pastor Rich edifies us anew with the wonderful, subversive love of Christ. With clarity, wisdom, and wit, he reminds us that God's ways are the ways of life, joy, love, and peace—the truly good life."

—DANAI GURIRA, actress, playwright, and activist

"The Sermon on the Mount stands on the universal scales as the most world-transforming sermon ever delivered, but it's also the most profound agenda for personal discipleship. What I hadn't quite grasped until I read Rich Villodas's book is that it acts in both of these ways, because this teaching is entirely autobiographical on Jesus's part. Rich is really telling a biography of Jesus—Divine One who not only clears the way, teaches the way, and shows the way—but *is* the Way. The path is narrow because it is only as wide as the person of Christ. But it is big enough for everyone's unique journey of life because he is the saviour of all. We know it isn't enough to give instruction manuals—people need maps. It's not sufficient to distribute handbooks—we need guides. This biography of the Jesus Way reset me on his way again. I hope and pray it sets and resets you on the Way. But my real hope is that it would become all our autobiographies. This book won't just do you good; it will do the world good."

—ARCHBISHOP JUSTIN WELBY, Archbishop of Canterbury

THE
NARROW
PATH

THE NARROW PATH

How the
Subversive Way of Jesus
Satisfies Our Souls

RICH VILLODAS

WATERBROOK

Published in the United States by WaterBrook, an imprint of Random House, a division of Penguin Random House LLC.

WATERBROOK and colophon are registered trademarks of Penguin Random House LLC.

Library of Congress Cataloging-in-Publication Data
Names: Villodas, Rich, author.
Title: The narrow path: how the subversive way of Jesus satisfies our souls / Rich Villodas.
Description: First edition. | Colorado Springs, Colo. : WaterBrook, [2024] | Includes bibliographical references.
Identifiers: LCCN 2023046526 | ISBN 9780593444276 (hardcover; acid-free paper) | ISBN 9780593444283 (ebook)
Subjects: LCSH: Jesus Christ—Person and offices. | Jesus Christ—Teachings. | Jesus Christ—Significance.
Classification: LCC BT203 .V55 2024 | DDC 232.9/54—dc23/eng20231205
LC record available at https://lccn.loc.gov/2023046526

Printed in the United States of America on acid-free paper

waterbrookmultnomah.com

2 4 6 8 9 7 5 3 1

First Edition

Book design by Elizabeth A. D. Eno

Most WaterBrook books are available at special quantity discounts for bulk purchase for premiums, fundraising, and corporate and educational needs by organizations, churches, and businesses. Special books or book excerpts also can be created to fit specific needs. For details, contact specialmarketscms@penguinrandomhouse.com.

For New Life Fellowship.
It's a joy to be on the narrow path with you.

Enter through the narrow gate. For wide is the gate and broad is the road that leads to destruction, and many enter through it. But small is the gate and narrow the road that leads to life, and only a few find it.

Matthew 7:13–14

CONTENTS

Introduction   xi

PART ONE: Understanding the Narrow Path

1   Unexpected Disaster (the Broad Path)   3
2   Unexpected Happiness   18
3   Unexpected Righteousness   33

INTERLUDE: Prayer and the Narrow Path   43

PART TWO: Walking the Narrow Path

4   Our Witness   49
5   Our Anger   61
6   Our Words   74
7   Our Desires   87
8   Our Money   99
9   Our Anxiety   115
10   Our Judgments   129
11   Our Decisions   144
12   Our Enemies   159

Afterword: Practicing Obedience   171
Acknowledgments   181
Notes   183

INTRODUCTION

I have come to love the world of Harry Potter. (For those of you who don't share this sentiment, please don't close this book.) One of my favorite scenes is from *Harry Potter and the Goblet of Fire*. A wizard named Mr. Weasley borrows a tent from a friend named Perkins while attending a larger-than-life sporting event. From the outside, it looks like a regular backyard tent that could fit two or three people. But Perkins, a fellow wizard, has charmed the tent, making it drastically larger on the inside. When Harry walks with Mr. Weasley's children through the narrow entryway, they find themselves in a three-room flat, with bunk beds, a kitchen, and a bathroom to boot. It's far more spacious than anyone expected.

When I think about the teachings of Jesus, especially in the Sermon on the Mount, this charmed tent comes to mind. The path of Jesus is most certainly narrow, as we will come to see, but it has been charmed, so to speak, with the ever-expanding life of God. At first Jesus's words seem constraining and restrictive, but—like with Mr. Weasley's tent—hidden within them is unimaginable power. As we enter, we discover a spaciousness for the soul that is difficult to experience from the outside. Yes, the path is narrow, but as we walk on it, we find ourselves living the kind of life we yearn for: one filled with love, joy, and peace.

In our culture, *narrow* is a negative term. It's used to describe closed-minded, stubborn, holier-than-thou people. You've encountered them, yes? Maybe you've seen them shouting at people at the local park who are holding picket signs that have John 3:16 on them. Or maybe the shouting comes in the form of an ALL CAPS Facebook tirade. To be narrow is not something we aspire to; it's a characteristic to avoid. Not so with Jesus. Please hear me out.

The narrow way of Jesus gets to the core of what it means to be human, what it means to love well. It focuses our energy on what truly leads to the good life: a spacious kind of existence that makes room for God and others.

Admittedly, the narrow path is rarely taken because it demands much of us. As the renown German theologian Dietrich Bonhoeffer said, "When Christ calls a man, he bids him come and die."[1] But you and I also understand something intuitively: Things that matter most never come easy. The greater the demand, the deeper the payoff. The greater the challenge, the more profound the joy when it is met. The higher the mountain, the deeper the satisfaction when it is summited. The more we die to ourselves and yield to Jesus, the more we come alive. This is the paradox of the Jesus Way.

Jesus wants you to experience the thrill and satisfaction

of the narrow way. The question is, Are you settling for less? This book aims to do two things:

1. Remind you that Jesus's narrow path offers the life you truly desire.

2. Help you stay on the path so you can experience the deep fulfillment Jesus alone offers.

If there's one place in Scripture that explains the narrow path, it's the Sermon on the Mount, Jesus's most famous set of teachings in Matthew 5–7. For the duration of this book, we will unpack the major teachings of his sermon. Let's pause briefly to reorient ourselves to this well-known (but often misunderstood) message.

The Sermon on the Mount

Eye for an eye. Salt of the earth. Light of the world. Let your yes be yes. Do not judge. Lead us not into temptation. Daily bread.

If you survey the average person walking down a street and ask them if they've ever heard these phrases, most will say yes. But if you ask where these phrases are found, you might hear crickets.

All these words and phrases are found in the Sermon on the Mount, which is essentially the best TED Talk ever given. The great leaders, preachers, and poets of history have been shaped by this message—everyone from Gandhi to Martin Luther King, Jr.

Name any historic speech and you'll find that Jesus's sermon outweighs them all. It's what the Declaration of Independence is to the United States, what Martin Luther King, Jr.'s "I Have a Dream" speech was to the civil rights movement, and then some. Everything that's been written or spoken pales in comparison to these soul-healing, world-changing, God-glorifying words of Jesus.

Invitation and Inventory

How you approach this sermon changes everything. If you see it as an instructional manual for salvation, every time you fail to live up to Jesus's words, you will question whether God is for you. Don't miss this: The sermon is not how we *achieve* salvation; it's how we *demonstrate* it. Those who have truly been transformed by Jesus resist the cultural norms around them. Thus, this sermon is a litmus test to help us assess whether we are following Jesus or someone else. In this way, the sermon is invitation and inventory. It invites us into a different way of seeing, hearing, and being. We were called to confound, confront, and convert a world out of darkness and into the peace-giving, love-animating, joy-fulfilling reign of God—not in our effort alone, but in the grace of God so generously poured out for us.

This sermon also prompts us to take inventory of our thoughts, words, and actions to see if they align with Jesus's glorious vision. Consider some of the sermon's major themes:

- *How can I forgive someone who hurt me?*

- *Am I serving God or money?*

- *Is trust or anxiety shaping my life?*

- *Can my word be taken at face value?*

- *Do I bless those who curse me?*

- *Do I have sexual integrity?*

As we examine these teachings, you might conclude that Jesus's path makes no sense. And you would be right. In the eyes of the world, Jesus's wisdom is nonsense—totally counterintuitive to cultural norms. But for those like me (and billions of others) who are weary of anchoring their lives in the unfulfilling promises of the surrounding culture, Jesus offers a better way. A narrow path. The life you and I desperately want but struggle to attain.

Choosing the narrow path requires trusting that Jesus knows what's best for you, even when it conflicts with your assumptions and expectations. Like the prophet Isaiah once said,

> "For my thoughts are not your thoughts,
>   neither are your ways my ways,"
>   declares the LORD.
> "As the heavens are higher than the earth,
>   so are my ways higher than your ways
>   and my thoughts than your thoughts."
>   (Isaiah 55:8–9)

The Journey Ahead

Unless we begin to take Jesus's words to our hearts and bodies, the faith we profess will not lead to the wholeness we desire. This book, then, is my attempt to narrow our vision once again, to help us set our lives in a particular direction, to strip off what has weighed us down, and to rediscover what it means to follow Jesus.

We will explore ancient themes that show up every day of our lives. In the process, what we will discover is that the key to a fulfilling, vibrant life is found in a radical narrow path—one that is not usually taken. We will discover that as we get on the narrow path, a new kind of spaciousness will be experienced: a spaciousness that can be realized only by stepping into what seems like a confined space.

We will also discover how subversive the way of Jesus is. His teachings undermine the prevailing notions of wisdom and power in his first-century context, and in ours as well. We will be surprised to learn that what the world prizes, Jesus devalues, and what Jesus applauds, the world rejects. As we pay close attention to his surprising perspectives, we will find ourselves living in a freedom that the world can't give, or take away.

All right, let's dive in to the best message ever preached by the wisest human who ever lived.

Part One

UNDERSTANDING
THE NARROW PATH

UNEXPECTED DISASTER
(THE BROAD PATH)

Have you ever been scuba diving? I haven't. But—
and I say this with more enthusiasm than I should—
I have snorkeled a few times, thank you very much.
On one of our wedding-anniversary trips, Rosie and I
looked up various excursions in Hawaii. I did extensive research, hoping to get in touch with the risk-taking part of
my personality. I watched a bunch of scuba videos on You-
Tube, finding inspiration and giving myself pep talks under
my breath. This was short-lived when I found a simple chart
outlining the differences between scuba diving and snorkeling. Suddenly I was jolted back to reality as the risk-taking
version of myself hid like a frightened cuttlefish.

I learned that scuba diving can cause something called
nitrogen narcosis, which is essentially like being drunk underwater. Or your equipment can fail. While diving, you're
also at risk of pulmonary embolism, which occurs when a

blood clot blocks the arteries in your lungs, causing dizziness, shortness of breath, and chest pain. Yeah, no thanks.

So I decided to snorkel. When you snorkel, you get sunburned, and, of course, I forgot to apply sunscreen and ended up with a scalded back. But at least I lived to tell the story.

The snorkeling excursion went well. I saw a handful of fish at a safe distance and came up for a quick break when I swallowed a bit of water through my tube. A few days later, I watched more scuba videos, hoping to muster the courage to take the dive. But my internal resistance was real. Cognitively, I knew a beautiful world awaited me in the depths, but I chose life on the surface, where things felt safe and predictable.

What does any of this have to do with the narrow path of Jesus? Many of us *want* to go deeper, but we find ourselves spiritually treading water on the surface. We try to live like Christian amphibians—half in, half out—but Jesus wants *all* of us, or, put differently, to give us all of himself. However, he knows nothing of half-hearted discipleship. His invitation is to follow him fully or not at all, using the metaphor of a road: "Enter through the narrow gate. For wide is the gate and broad is the road that leads to destruction, and many enter through it. But small is the gate and narrow the road that leads to life, and only a few find it" (Matthew 7:13–14).

As profound as Jesus is, I love his simplicity. There are two paths to take: the narrow path or the broad one. The narrow path is the cruciform way of Jesus that leads to renewal and healing. Naturally, we're interested in the "road that leads to life," so what holds us back? If we're honest, it's the cost. As G. K. Chesterton wrote, "The Christian ideal has not been tried and found wanting. It has been found difficult; and left untried."[1]

We're afraid following Jesus will summon us to a new way of life we don't prefer or can't sustain.

We keep Jesus at a "safe" distance because we assume following him leads to a joyless, confined existence of re-pressing our desires and taking on a mechanical, religious persona.

We avoid Jesus's narrow path because we believe we will have to deny our yearning for sexual intimacy, surrender all our dreams, and go to multiple church services a week.

We're afraid of what others will think if we *really* follow Jesus. We don't want to be religious fanatics.

We avoid the narrow path because it requires facing ourselves—looking in the mirror with honesty and vulner-ability.

I've wondered these things too.

To journey through a narrow path takes time. It requires you and me to slow down. At some point, we all must face the parts of ourselves we don't like. And you know what? Sometimes it's easier to avoid this invitation altogether. Maybe you're afraid of going deep because seeing more of Jesus means him seeing more of *you*. If that's what you're feeling, you're not alone.

As I've carefully observed Jesus's interactions with peo-ple in Scripture and felt his presence in my own life, I've discovered time and time again that Jesus isn't repelled by human brokenness; he's attracted to it.

As a nineteen-year-old, just a few months into my rela-tionship with Jesus, I read a book on his holy presence. For the first time, I realized I could set aside the self-protective façade that ensnared me into a performance-driven life and addictive behavior, and I wept. I wrote in my new leather-bound journal the various secrets I'd been carrying. After each sentence, I'd look over my shoulder, fearing someone was hovering over me like a schoolteacher during a final exam. In what felt like holy angst, I sensed the presence of God within me. I recalled the tenderness of Jesus in the gospel stories, which I was learning for the first time. I continued to name the places in my soul I'd been hiding from God, others, and myself. And I found grace and mercy. Tenderness and compassion. Peace and joy.

Despite that powerful experience, I still lose my way from time to time. Maybe, like me, you've had seasons when you've been busy or distracted, content to give God the leftovers. In such seasons, Jesus invites you and me to return to the narrow path.

Only Two Paths . . . *Really, Jesus?*

Jesus's teaching about two paths—a broad way that leads to destruction, and a narrow way that leads to life—is a bit intimidating. It immediately prompts various questions:

What does the narrow path look like?
What does the broad path look like?
How do I know which path I'm on?

We will spend ample time exploring these important questions, but before we do, can we take a moment to name the elephant in the room? What I mean is, isn't Jesus oversimplifying life when he gives us just two paths? Isn't life more nuanced and complex than this? It sounds reductionistic. It confounds us. It even offends us.

In other places in the Gospels, Jesus masterfully outmaneuvers all kinds of ethical and theological conundrums by responding to questions from an angle no one was expecting. But there's no nuance here. There are two paths: broad or narrow. But before we set aside this teaching, let us acknowledge that Jesus is in good company when he suggests two ways.

He's in the company of Yahweh in the Old Testament when two paths—death and life—are placed before the people of God (see Deuteronomy 30:19).

He's in the company of Master Yoda, who preached on the two paths of the Force: the light side and the dark side (kidding, partially).

He's in the company of Morpheus, who offered the blue pill and the red pill to Neo in *The Matrix*. Plenty of teachers, religious or not, present two divergent paths and invite their followers to choose one.

When Jesus offers two paths, he's being clear, not cruel. He's leading us to life—freeing us from the paralysis of decision fatigue.

When most people read Jesus's words about the narrow and the broad paths, it's through the lens of good morality versus bad morality, or perhaps the afterlife. The narrow path is the path "good" people take; the broad way is the preferred route of "bad" sinners. The narrow path is the avenue toward heaven, while the broad way is the road to hell. But that outlook is not what Jesus has in mind. Naturally, the path you choose now has a bearing on eternity, but Jesus also desires to form us *today*. To bear witness to the radical nature of life in his kingdom. The broad path is life outside Jesus's rule and way; the narrow path is life submitted to him and his subversive wisdom.

Am I on the Broad Path?

The question burning in our minds is likely this: *How do I know I'm on the broad path?* The Sermon on the Mount helps answer that question, letting us see that it's possible to serve God without walking with him. In other words, we can be on the broad path without knowing it. Jesus's words are a penetrating analysis of the human problem. I can't say it enough: God wants to form the entirety of us, and a large part of that formation requires us to name our false assumptions about him and the "good life." Let's simplify the problems before us in three statements. You may be on the broad path if . . .

1. You believe God cares about only your behavior, not your heart (moralism).
2. You have a superficial vision of what "the good life" is (success-ism).
3. You see spirituality as just you and God (individualism).

The convergence of these three problems serves as the root of our spiritual brokenness. They constitute the broad way—the path taken by most.

Moralism

I remember offering a series of pastoral counseling sessions to a member of our community. Let's call him Jeremy (not his real name). Jeremy, a thirty-seven-year-old high school teacher, found himself caring for his aging father. He shared about his growing fatigue and simmering resentment due to all he was carrying at work and at home. His father needed *some* extra help, but, realistically, if Jeremy scaled back a bit, things would have been fine. Jeremy lamented that he couldn't take a Sabbath, and the notion of self-care felt impossible. He wanted guidance on practices of prayer to help him better carry this weight. So far, so good.

By the third session, I started to dig deeper. I asked if he would be able to take a weekend off from supporting his dad to get some needed rest. He immediately listed all the reasons that wouldn't work. I pressed him.

"Jeremy, what if you told your father that two weeks from now, you'll be away?"

"I can try, but I don't know if that will work," he responded. I pressed in further. I stood up with a dry-erase marker in hand and walked to the whiteboard.

"What internal messages might be fueling your actions?" After seven to eight minutes of silence, we started capturing what was swirling inside him. We ended up naming three internalized messages:

1. *If I don't help, I'm a bad son.*

2. *My needs don't matter.*

3. *Saying no to my father means I'm violating the fifth commandment about honoring father and mother.*

We looked at the whiteboard together, and I offered some alternative perspectives that challenged his internal messages. Two weeks later, he took a weekend off and was miserable. We processed some more a week later, and we both noticed some positive shifts in his perspective.

We summarized the lesson we'd been slowly discovering with these words on the whiteboard: "Focusing on my external behavior without interior examination creates resentment." (By *interior examination,* I'm referring to the prayerful practice of examining the values, messages, motives, and feelings we harbor.)

Jeremy could have lived his entire life in bondage to a set of internalized messages that compelled him to unrelentingly serve his parents. And this possibility of bondage lives in all of us.

Jesus is never about adjusting behavior alone. He cares about *who we are becoming,* not just what we do. He rejects a spirituality that doesn't transform our hearts. To adjust our behavior—even in positive directions—without interior examination will enslave us.

Said differently, we can do all the right things but never examine why or how we should do them. I know what it's like to help others not out of deep concern but to avoid their displeasure. I'm familiar with speaking truth not because I'm compelled by God to do so but because I'm afraid of being rejected by people I respect. I've been an expert at saying yes to all kinds of invitations not because I feel led by God but because I'll be seen in a positive light.

The broad path is content with believing the "right" things and doing the "right" stuff, assuming that's all Jesus wants. But a deeper look into our motivations is necessary for cultivating life with God.

This deeper look can be accessed through some simple questions: *Why do we do what we do? Why do we pray? Why do we serve others?* It's possible to live many years without taking time to explore the complex motives that energize our decisions and ways of life. When we do, it's common to unearth fear, shame, pride, and performance.

Unfortunately, few people take the time to sift their own motivations.

It's easier to tackle addictive behavior without exploring the deeper woundedness we seek to soothe. It's easier to work nonstop without pausing to examine the ways we are trying to secure love or attain status. Slowing down—looking within—is difficult. Jesus, however, calls us to search our own hearts.

You can't know God deeply while being a stranger to yourself. I meet many people who say they know God but who don't know themselves. When Jesus addresses matters of lust or anger in the Sermon on the Mount, he's naming this reality. He doesn't let us live on the surface. He calls us deeper. Behavior modification without interior examination eventually leads to spiritual desolation.

Success-ism

We also avoid the narrow path of Jesus because we believe there's a better option out there—one that offers more fun, freedom, and fulfillment. Close your eyes for a moment and reflect on what the "good life" looks like. What comes to mind? Chances are, for many of us, the good life means health, a beautiful home, a successful career, a loving family, lots of time for leisure, and the absence of pain. It's certainly what *I* think about!

These indicators of the good life are wonderful. We all want good health, a nice home, success in vocational ventures, loving relationships, and time for relaxation. But is the good life we envision drawn from the American dream or from the kingdom of God? To orient one's life around God (in our case, the message of the Sermon on the Mount) doesn't mean that this vision of the good life must be totally set aside. However, it does require us to ask ourselves honestly, *What is really shaping the trajectory of my life?*

The broad path is the path of our own making, which is why it's the preferred route. We set the course. We determine what success is. We create the scorecard. But Jesus doesn't leave us on our own. He confronts us and invites us onto a path that most people aren't excited to choose. And why are they not likely to choose it? Because it doesn't come with the bells and whistles of our cultural notions of what's good.

Jesus understands this personally.

Immediately after his baptism, where the Father affirms, "You are my Son, whom I love; with you I am well pleased" (Mark 1:11), Jesus enters the wilderness to be tempted by the devil. Each temptation—turning stones into bread, bowing to Satan, and jumping off the temple—is designed to warp Jesus's view of the good life. The devil offers a vision that prizes instant gratification over disciplined dependence, power over servanthood, applause over humility.

The devil, in his own way, tries to divert Jesus from the narrow path. Jesus must choose: Is he a messiah who thinks about himself over others? Does he live for power, or does he lay it down for others? Does he live for the applause of people, or rest in the affirmation of his Father? Jesus chooses the narrow path, which deprives him of food, power, and approval—at least for a time.

What's your vision of the good life? What is your family's

summary of a life well lived? What's your understanding of a good world? If you're not sure, look at how you spend your money and time. What are you perpetually chasing? What are your deepest desires and goals? Where does your ambition surface? These questions help show if you're being formed into the image of Jesus or a copy of the fallen world around you.

Jesus invites you and me to reimagine what a good life truly is. Look at the lives transformed in the Gospels because of Jesus's alternative road. Observe the freedom that came from his generous forgiveness. Contemplate those who found solace in him—people who had spent their whole lives feeling spiritually and socially homeless. Picture the multitudes who were healed because of his compassion.

Just think what you, in the power of his Spirit, can accomplish throughout your life! Redefining the good life may seem like a loss at first, but it ultimately yields the kind of significance you yearn for—a life that blesses others and avoids the popular trappings of our world.

Individualism

"You gotta do you." That's the advice I overheard from a young man talking on the phone, strutting along a sidewalk in Queens, New York, where I live. His words capture a maxim adopted by many: Just be yourself. "Doing you" can be a necessary correction for someone too tangled up in what others think. It can be an expression of self-care for someone who has neglected their own needs. But many times, "doing you" is just another way to choose the broad path of spiritual individualism.

This problem might be the most deceptive, convincing us that we love God even while we neglect our neighbor.

As an example, consider the notion of American freedom, which says, "My freedom is *mine* to enjoy." Contrast this with Christian freedom, which implies, "My freedom is for the purpose of serving my neighbor" (see Galatians 5:13).

Christian freedom is about service. The freedom so often espoused in our culture is about self. Christian freedom is found in God, my neighbor, and myself (in that order). Modern freedom is oriented around the unholy trinity: me, myself, and I.

Our love for our neighbor—especially the neighbor who is very different from us—is proof of our love for God. Our theology, no matter how good, becomes irrelevant and idolatrous when it's not used in service of loving God and neighbor.

No one understands this better than Jesus. In one scene, he is approached by the Pharisees, a group of rigidly devoted religious leaders in Jesus's day: "Teacher, which is the greatest commandment in the Law?" (Matthew 22:36).

Jesus, sensing a verbal trap, quotes from Deuteronomy 6, "*Hear,* O Israel: The LORD our God, the LORD is one. Love the LORD your God with all your heart and with all your soul and with all your strength" (verses 4–5). Then, right after referencing this well-known scripture, he adds something to it: "'Love the Lord your God with all your heart and with all your soul and with all your mind and with all your strength.' The second is this: 'Love your neighbor as yourself.' There is no commandment greater than these" (Mark 12:30–31).

The question was, "Which is the greatest commandment in the Law?" Jesus cites two. "There is no *commandment* greater than *these*." Now, for you English teachers out there, you may notice the grammatical problem with that sentence. A single commandment should have a singular modifier. We expect Jesus to say, "There is no commandment greater than *this*."

It's grammatically incorrect but spiritually perceptive.

In Jesus's mind, these two commandments are inseparable. It is impossible to separate loving God and loving others. It is impossible to separate our personal relationship with God from our personal relationships with those around us. I'm aware of this multiple nights a week at our family dinner table.

Before every meal, we offer a word of loving thanks to God for the food we are about to eat (you know, standard Christian stuff). We also pray for those in our neighborhood who might be homeless and hungry. To pray for those who are hungry can be an act of love but also a subtle way of escaping the harder work of practical love. One way I'm trying to help my children live into Jesus's commandments is to point them to simple ways to be generous, like donating money or volunteering time to serve the poor. It's a simple way to help them (and ourselves as their parents!) see the connection Jesus makes between love for God and love for neighbor.

These two commandments mirror one another. How you love God is how you love your neighbor, and how you love your neighbor is how you love God.

Let me say it again: How you love others is how you love God. This is one of the reasons many are giving up on the church. A faith that purports to love God but mistreats others is a farce. Evidence of whether our character is being formed by Jesus is found in the quality of our love.

Throughout the Sermon on the Mount (and in multiple places elsewhere in the Gospels), Jesus defines the broad path as a lifestyle that doesn't see love of God and love of neighbor as a singular thread. Tragically, there are many Christians on the broad path. When the church refuses to love our neighbor—whether it be our gay, black, white, immigrant, poor, Democrat, or Republican neighbor—we are traveling on a path that doesn't lead to life.

Although it's easy to drift onto the broad path—to succumb to moralism, success-ism, and individualism—there is good news. There is another path available to us. Jesus invites us onto the narrow path, and no matter how long we've deviated from it, we're always welcome. That's what this book is all about.

The Promise of the Narrow Path

The narrow path is not about the number of people who will end up in heaven; it's about the number of people who will allow themselves to be formed by the subversive and, ultimately, redemptive way of Jesus.

To the world, this path seems rigid, impractical, and uncomfortable (to be sure, it will be at times), but like a sea diver adjusting to the heavy pressure of an underwater existence, if we submit to the process, Jesus will show us a world of wonders we never thought possible! We can stay on the surface, safe and dry, peering into the water, catching blurry glimpses of the beauty underneath . . . *or* we can dive in and immerse ourselves in a glorious realm.

I know firsthand how terrifying it is to take the deep dive, so let's go on this journey together. Thankfully, the narrow path is for the spiritually hungry, not the elite. If you choose to follow Jesus down this path, he will meet you in unexpected ways. Yes, he may tear down the false self you've built, but rather than your identity being erased, you will become your full and true self. You'll discover life as an easy yoke and light burden. You'll encounter the grace of God that empowers you to live a truly significant life.

Is this easy? Not one bit. Is it worth it? As Jesus puts it, you'll discover life "to the full" (John 10:10).

Are you ready? One step at a time. Here we go.

2

UNEXPECTED HAPPINESS

The *New York Times* published an article titled "Yale's Most Popular Class Ever: Happiness." The article begins,

On Jan. 12, a few days after registration opened at Yale for Psych 157, Psychology and the Good Life, roughly 300 people had signed up. Within three days, the figure had more than doubled. After three more days, about 1,200 students, or nearly one-fourth of Yale undergraduates, were enrolled.[1]

What sparked such a massive response? Something living inside those students—inside all of us—yearns for the good life. The thing is, long before Yale launched a happiness course, Jesus began the Sermon on the Mount with a primer on true happiness, or what he called *blessedness*. His sermon's short snippets on true happiness are often called the Beatitudes.

The Blessed Life

So, what *is* happiness all about, according to Jesus's beatitudes? Spoiler alert: It's not what most people think. Jesus doesn't primarily describe emotions or feelings; instead, he describes a subversive and surprising way of life—an upside-down existence that upsets our understanding of who's on top and who's on bottom.

In the opening words of Jesus's manifesto, he doesn't mince words. He goes for the jugular from the onset. He challenges and critiques prevailing wisdom and social convention. He details what the good life truly is and who the blessed ones truly are.

Notice that rather than having a list of to-dos, he begins his sermon by letting us know who is blessed. By starting there, he clarifies that those in his kingdom don't work *for* blessing but *from* blessing. Jesus's disciples don't have to *seek* blessing; they are *already* blessed by God. Jesus seems to know something about the human condition: We can live a lifetime climbing a particular ladder of success or blessedness, only to find out the ladder we climbed was placed on the wrong wall. In kindness, Jesus announces what we are all looking for: joy.

Who Are the Blessed Ones?

To be blessed is to be accepted and approved by God, whether or not circumstances seem to confirm or deny it. Blessedness produces unassailable happiness and joy regardless of circumstances.

Who are the people we most want to be like? They're usually those who are most fortunate, happy, and prosperous. In a word, we want to be like those we deem as blessed. But Jesus takes this culturally loaded word and flips the script. Why? Because humanity has been seduced into a vision of the good life that's based on good physical health, ample money, positivity, acclaim, and minimal challenges.

Jesus turns it all around, explaining that the most fortunate people are those who are socially disregarded, are deemed unworthy by the dominant culture, and recognize their deep need for God.

To follow Jesus is to have a radically different scorecard of success and significance. God's rejection of our cultural brand of success (wealth, health, power, influence, and so on) upsets many who base their lives on it. It's not that God despises people who are comfortable; it's that he knows the benefit of spiritual disruption, especially when prevailing assumptions about the good life are dangerous.

This disruption is desperately needed. As someone who puts too much stock in what people think about me, I have subconsciously attached the good life to the avoidance of conflict. If no one is mad at me, I believe I'm doing well. For Jesus, however, conflict is sometimes necessary for the sake of love.

For other people, the good life is tied to enjoyment and entertainment. To put up with drudgery in the workplace or at home is a sign that one's life lacks goodness. Even more, the good life can be reduced to influence and power. Admiration and respect become the goal.

So, what does the good life look like in Jesus's kingdom?

Let's briefly explore each beatitude, then consider its implication for our lives.

Blessed Are the Poor in Spirit

Blessed are the poor in spirit, for theirs is the kingdom of heaven. (Matthew 5:3)

In Matthew's gospel, Jesus uses the phrase "poor in spirit." In Luke's gospel, it's the phrase "you who are poor" (6:20). Scholars note that Luke wrote with the *material* poor in mind, while Matthew meant the *spiritually* poor. Both must be considered.

To be spiritually poor is to acknowledge our profound need for God's life and love. It's a confession of inadequacy. Over the years, I've heard people say that religion in general (and Christianity in particular) is for weak people who need a crutch to help them get through life. I remember having a conversation with someone who mentioned this need for religion's "crutch." I told him that I disagreed with his portrayal of Christianity. As he prepared to state his case, I told him that Christianity was more than a crutch for the weak. It's a wheelchair, a gurney. It's a hospital. Better yet, it's a hearse. Christianity doesn't say you have a limp and therefore offers a crutch; it announces that we are dead and in need of a power outside ourselves to bring us to life. That's what it means to be poor in spirit.

The word *poor* is a translation of the Hebrew word that carries the basic idea of "lacking." In Psalms, when someone says they are poor, it sometimes denotes a lack of property or resources. However, more often it refers to *spiritual* neediness. Psalms uses the word *poor* more than thirty times to describe those who recognize they need God.

Jesus says the kingdom belongs to such people. The only condition required to inherit this kingdom is a recognition that, apart from him, we are impoverished. As Jesus says in John 15:5, "Apart from me you can do nothing."

Blessed Are Those Who Mourn

Blessed are those who mourn, for they will be comforted. (Matthew 5:4)

The world says blessed are those without any problems. Blessed are those who always see the bright side of things. Not so fast. In Jesus's kingdom, mourning—not merrymaking—brings blessing. How can this be?

To mourn means to carry our grief to God. To lament. To refuse to sugarcoat life. It's authenticity, looking honestly at the brokenness of the world and the brokenness of our lives.

As a college student, one of my assignments in a spiritual-formation class was to write an eight-page paper on grief and loss. It was a painful undertaking because it was the first time I allowed myself to consider the losses I experienced throughout childhood (including various betrayals of trust, as well as losing family members to premature deaths). As I processed these things, my grief felt overwhelming.

Even today, working through past pain is difficult for me, but I have met God while doing so. I can be easily formed by a world that numbs pain and moves quickly to the next thing. But the joy available through the narrow path of the kingdom doesn't come by eliminating grief. To cut out grief from our lives is to crush our joy as well. We can't numb our emotions without compromising everything else.

Jesus doesn't want us to wallow in grief; instead, he gives us access to the comfort of God. He helps us become the kind of people who demonstrate God's care to a bruised world. That is why one of the great practices of spirituality is reading through Psalms regularly, even the ones that don't seem to reflect our current emotional states. As we open ourselves to the prayers and songs of mourning, we are given windows into the grief-stricken world we inhabit and are invited to join God in working for its healing.

Blessed Are the Meek

Blessed are the meek, for they will inherit the earth. (Matthew 5:5)

Meekness is not weakness; it's power under control. It refuses to be shaped by aggressive possessiveness and embraces humble trust. The meek are not self-deprecating, timid people. On the contrary, Jesus says these people will inherit the earth. They are victors, not victims.

Once again, Jesus reverses life as we know it. Those who will inherit the earth—which is shorthand for "the life to come"—will be those who are now powerless and oppressed. This is not a call to be passive in the face of injustice (as the next beatitude makes clear); it's a hopeful vision of tomorrow that directs our work today.

In Jesus's eyes, the poor, the abused, the oppressed, the marginalized, and the disinherited have special status in his kingdom. In the same way his cruciform life led to a glorious resurrection, those suffering now are promised a glorious inheritance. That is the mysterious, justice-seeking love of God.

Although gentleness is prized in God's kingdom, few things sound more foolish to city dwellers like me. If you've spent any time in a big city, you soon find out that if you're going to survive, you need to be aggressive. When I play basketball in Brooklyn, I don't huddle up my team and say, "On three, gentleness!" When I take the subway during rush hour in Manhattan, gentleness gets me nowhere. If I drive in the city gently navigating through traffic, I'll get eaten alive.

We are trained to think that if we're going to make it, we have to be aggressive. Yet in the kingdom of God, the way of gentleness is what will heal the world.

Blessed Are Those Who Hunger and Thirst for Righteousness

> Blessed are those who hunger and thirst for righteousness, for they will be filled. (Matthew 5:6)

Hunger and thirst are not typical signs of blessedness, but once again, Jesus's ways are not our ways. The people Jesus has in mind can be explained as those who are deprived of justice (a good translation of the word righteousness) and those who dispense it.

God delights to bless those who long for justice. Jesus

says, "They will be filled." This speaks to the ultimate victory of God: when he ends injustice, oppression, and evil once and for all. One day this world, writhing in the agony of justice, will be healed in full. This is good news for those trapped in human trafficking. For those subjected to corrupt politicians. For the person imprisoned in an abusive relationship. In all these cases, people who long for things to be made right—after having been on the receiving end of so much wrong—will be filled with the satisfaction of seeing God judge evil and bring about justice.

Additionally, this blessing is conferred on those who lift their voices and join their lives to the lives of people longing for a better world. Jesus's first sermon in the book of Luke (see chapter 4) is about good news for the overlooked. The gospel liberates the vulnerable, the poor, and the mistreated. It brings individual, interpersonal, and institutional wholeness.

This beatitude reminds us that one day God will make everything sad untrue. A day is coming when he will exalt the lowly and lower the exalted—when he will end oppression and all exploitation. Who, then, are the blessed ones? In short, the ones who seek to make things right like God does.

Blessed Are the Merciful

Blessed are the merciful, for they will be shown mercy. (Matthew 5:7)

We live in a world dominated by meanness, not mercy. Thus, it makes sense why Jesus connects happiness (blessedness) and mercy. Mercy means to come to the aid of the needy. As this practice gets embodied in our lives, we become reflections of the Father, who delights in showing mercy (see Micah 7:18). God is the father who runs after his children after they make a mess of their lives. God is the healer who restores the sick with his mighty touch. God is the one who forgives our sin and doesn't bring it up again. Mercy. Pure mercy.

This beatitude puzzles people because it seems to suggest that only those who are merciful can receive mercy. This need not cause confusion. God in Christ is an unending fount of mercy and grace. God's mercy arrives long before we consciously seek it. It is present even while we remain absent to its transforming power. It is prevenient—it moves toward us before we return the favor. God's mercy comes first. Then, after living within that gift of mercy, we learn to pass it on to others. Priest and theologian Ron Rolheiser captures this well in a conversation he had with an old priest. One night he asked,

> "If you had your priesthood to live over again, would you do anything differently?" From a man so full of integrity, I fully expected that there would be no regrets. So his answer surprised me. Yes, he did have a regret, a major one, he said: "If I had my priesthood to do over again, I would be easier on people the next time. I wouldn't be so stingy with God's mercy, with the sacraments, with forgiveness. . . . I fear that I've been too hard on people. They have pain enough without me and the church laying further burdens on them. I should have risked God's mercy more!"[2]

What a great phrase: "I should have risked God's mercy more!"

Blessed Are the Pure in Heart

Blessed are the pure in heart, for they will see God. (Matthew 5:8)

Some years ago, I looked at the stars through a friend's telescope. It took me a while to see the constellations he was pointing out, but he kept encouraging me to focus. When I was finally able to discern the celestial outlines, a joy welled up within me. I needed something to help me focus and narrow my attention to see. That is what Jesus is saying with this beatitude.

To be pure in heart is to "will one thing," in the words of Søren Kierkegaard.[3] It's to say, like David in Psalm 27:4, "One thing I ask from the LORD, this only do I seek." To be pure in heart is what Mary (Martha's sister) does at the feet of Jesus. She sits at his feet, attentive to every word (see Luke 10:39). Jesus commends her by saying, "One thing is necessary. Mary has chosen the good portion" (verse 42, ESV).

Jesus's kingdom calls us to single-mindedness. Again, narrowness does not close our eyes to the real world; rather, like using a telescope, narrowing our focus *expands* our vision. Purity of heart tends to be seen through the lens of moralism, as in, "Don't let your heart be contaminated by the filth of world." Of course, as followers of Jesus, we do well to discern the things we watch and listen to, knowing we are always being formed by something. But the purity Jesus is primarily talking about here makes God the single focus of our hearts and affection.

God is distinct from his creation yet visible amid it. He wants you to see him in and through all things. That is what it means to be a mystic. Mysticism is usually associated with esoteric visions and strange experiences. But at the core of Christian mysticism is a growing ability—generated by grace—to see traces of God in the world. That is the good news of the kingdom: God makes himself accessible here and now. To see him, though, you must be pure in heart.

How do we do this? By beholding him in prayer and stillness. The pure in heart are more known for their God-attentiveness than their sin-avoidance. In fact, fixing our attention and affection on God is the most powerful strategy for defeating sin.

Blessed Are the Peacemakers

Blessed are the peacemakers, for they will be called children of God. (Matthew 5:9)

Peacemakers are those who work for right relationships at the expense of their comfort. We don't usually choose this route, nor do we understand what it really means. Jesus does *not* say, "Blessed are the peace*keepers*." What's the difference between peacekeeping and peacemaking?

Here's the distinction. Peace*keeping* tries not to rock the boat, avoids conflict, and is superficial. It ensures that no one gets upset. That's not real peace. When, out of fear, we avoid conflict and appease people, we are false peacemakers. Here are some everyday examples:

- You're upset with your spouse, who constantly comes home later after work. You say nothing, trying not to criticize, but inside you're stewing because you need help with the kids at the end of a long day. You're passive-aggressive and give the silent treatment. That's false peace.

- You hear co-workers slandering your boss. You disagree with them, but since you're afraid to speak up, you go along with it. You think, *I don't want to create an awkward moment.* That's false peace.

- Your boyfriend is irresponsible, but you feel bad for him. You say to yourself, *He's been through so much pain in his life. How can I add to that?* So you back down from telling him that his behavior is slowly killing your relationship, which then dies a slow death. That is false peace.

Here's the thing with peace*keeping:* sooner or later, it brings chaos—not peace—into your life. Peace*making* is quite different. Peacemakers don't avoid conflict; in fact, sometimes peacemaking *creates* it. We see this with Jesus. As the epitome of love, he wasn't always nice—at least not in the way modern people visualize niceness.

On several occasions, he burst into the temple and flipped tables over because poor, vulnerable people were being taken advantage of (see Matthew 21:12). When he saw the Pharisees putting yokes of religious condemnation on people, he confronted the religious leaders with harsh words.

As Jesus's life reveals, peacemaking is often met with resistance. Paradoxically, to make peace means entering a war. The peace of God uproots the exploitative schemes of evil, and that evil won't back down without a fight. Which leads us to Jesus's final beatitude—about persecution.

Blessed Are Those Who Are Persecuted Because of Righteousness

Blessed are those who are persecuted because of righteousness, for theirs is the kingdom of heaven. Blessed are you when people insult you, persecute you and falsely say all kinds of evil against you because of me. Rejoice and be glad, because great is your reward in heaven, for in the same way they persecuted the prophets who were before you. (Matthew 5:10–12)

This beatitude is not for the faint of heart. The world needs peacemakers, but to work for peace requires us to step into situations often possessed by anxious forces. This possession can lead to violence as people resist being called to a new way of living in the world—one that prevents them from preying upon the weak for their own gain.

Notice that Jesus says, "Blessed are those who are persecuted *because of righteousness*." He doesn't confer blessing on those persecuted for self-righteousness. Or religious zeal. Or anything else. It's easy to label all hardship a reward for "righteousness," even when our trouble is merely the result of stubbornness and pride. True persecution comes when we are mistreated because of a steadfast commitment to righteousness (justice). To be sure, walking with Jesus will turn some people against us. The good news is, such mistreatment is a blessing in the long run. Don't give up!

The Good Life

Okay, take a deep breath. That's a lot of cultural and psychological reordering Jesus is doing for us. Briefly, let's distill these eight blessings into three principles that show why following his narrow path leads to the good life—the *best* life.

First, **God blesses weakness over strength.** Reflect again on the words Jesus emphasizes: *poor, mourn, meek,* and *mercy.* These are unfamiliar to the power structures of our world. You'll never see a magazine spotlighting the Unfortunate 500 list of companies. No, you'll read about only the rich and powerful. In many cultures, mourning is a sign of weakness. Big boys don't cry, right? Those who are in touch with their pain and loss are often seen as inferior to those who push forward with grit. *Meekness* rhymes with *weakness,* so there you go with that one. Offering mercy is usually dismissed as political and social softness.

Jesus subverts this. Instead of the self-sufficient, it's those dependent on his power who are blessed. Those living with great tenderness and grace are the most fortunate. Those who reject the power plays of the world are especially close to God.

We also learn, second, that **the good life is directly tied**

to the quality of love we embody. Jesus's beatitudes insist that love is what makes life good. To hunger for justice and righteousness, to be peacemakers, to offer mercy—all these acts are expressions of love. In the kingdom of God, the happiest people are oriented around love, not accruing greater possessions or power. To walk in step with Jesus is to walk in the way of love. A love that seeks to bring reconciliation where there has been fragmentation. A love that rejoices over mercy, not resentment. A love that works to end injustice, refusing to stand by idly. That is, for Jesus, the path toward the life that satisfies our souls.

Finally, we learn from Jesus that **the life God blesses is cruciform in nature.** Jesus is clear that the blessed ones are not free from trouble. Rather, they *endure* trouble as they bear witness to Jesus's subversive path. I wish I could tell you that following Jesus always leads to unencumbered, comfortable lives of leisure. But as Jesus teaches in his beatitudes, the blessed life is connected to the cross. To pattern our lives after Christ requires death to our egos, our false selves, and the larger culture that incentivizes self-centeredness.

Here's the glorious news: The sign of the cross is a sign of God's coming vindication for all who choose the Jesus Way. As God raised Jesus from the dead, so, too, he will raise *you* from the dead. As God vindicated his Son, God will also vindicate those who choose the way of the Son.

So be of good cheer, dear friend. Following Jesus, even into discomfort, places you among the most blessed people on earth.

3

UNEXPECTED RIGHTEOUSNESS

If a good deed done is not posted on social media, did it really happen? If an act of generosity is not caught on camera and never goes viral, was it a worthwhile gesture? These questions, facetious as they seem, point out something I've observed in my own life: a deep desire to display my goodness to others. There's even a modern term for it: *virtue signaling*.

According to Jesus, this is an ancient struggle, a primal temptation. We long to be known and seen, but if we aren't careful, this longing can lead to a kind of performativity that corrodes the soul.

In Matthew 6—the center of the Sermon on the Mount—Jesus flips showy spirituality on its head: "Be careful not to practice your righteousness in front of others to be seen. . . . But when you give to the needy, do not let your left hand know what your right hand is doing" (verses 1, 3). Jesus reveals a key characteristic of his narrow path: hiddenness.

That is an important word for those who, like me, intuitively strive to be noticed. Can you relate? Social media has created (or perhaps revealed) the hunger within us to be seen. As some have aptly said, the current generation of young adults—and emerging ones—can be described as Generation Notification.

Each time we get notifications—those coveted red or blue circles with a number in them—dopamine releases in our brains. The cycle is hard to break. Even if a comment is negative, receiving one is still addicting because being seen is better than remaining invisible.

To be known and seen is one of our deepest longings. But left to our own devices (pun intended), we get stuck in a never-ending cycle of performative spirituality, where we seek to get from others what can be given only by God.

Jesus's warning to us, then, is not just good spirituality; it's good psychology. To be his disciple requires being a whole person, not merely doing religious things. What often stands in the way is a lack of self-awareness—not knowing our inner selves. How do we overcome this?

Good Versus Bad Self-Awareness

To combat the unrelenting desire to be seen by others, we are called by Jesus to hiddenness. Once again, the paradox of the kingdom of God is evident. The narrow path of Jesus says that if we want to be strong, we must be weak; if we want to be first, we must be last; if we want to be great, we must be least. It's the same pattern here: To be truly seen, we must be hidden.

This hiddenness is challenging because Jesus doesn't primarily mean hiddenness from the world; he means hiddenness from *ourselves*. To better understand this, it might be helpful to contrast good self-awareness with bad self-awareness.

Good self-awareness sees areas of our lives that are constraining us. It helps us name the forces that keep us from living free, full, and loving lives. Good self-awareness focuses on our reactions and triggers. It reflects on the things we've done and the things left undone. Good self-awareness leads to humility and invites us into a process of growth.

When Jesus says, "Do not let your left hand know what your right hand is doing" (Matthew 6:3), he invites you into a "holy unawareness."

Which leads me to the temptation of bad self-awareness. Self-awareness becomes damaging when the focus is on our righteousness. When we're caught up in our own goodness, living a self-congratulatory existence. Bad self-awareness fixates on our deeds and exaggerates our spiritual growth. There have been many times when I've obsessed over my progress.

When I exercise, I have a tendency to look in the mirror way more than I need to. After twenty-five push-ups, my chest feels like that of a professional bodybuilder, so I go to the mirror to confirm my suspicions (and am sorely disappointed each time). My tendency to document my growth roots me in despair or pride, depending on the day. In all this, I've discovered that the most mature people are not consumed with their fruitfulness, nor do they wallow in their failures.

The Performing Life

It's exhausting to live a life of performance. Jesus offers a better way. Aren't you tired of always having to be "on"?

Isn't it draining to work for constant approval? Do you ever feel as though God will be disappointed if you don't have everything in order?

Jesus doesn't lead us into a scrupulous spirituality in which we agonize over every decision. Rather, he calls us to examine the ground from which our good deeds grow. Why? So we don't entrap ourselves in self-righteousness or idolatry: self-righteousness because our goodness can cloud the grace of God; idolatrous because without knowing it, we worship acclaim from others instead of from God.

When our deeds are practiced in front of others, we forfeit the rewards we will receive from the Father. Instead of receiving commendation from God, we settle for admiration from people. Of course, Jesus is not saying that all recognition and reward is incongruent with life in the kingdom. He's clarifying that to live for it is folly. Applause from others, social media likes—it all fades quickly. Only the affirming word of the Father can fill our hearts.

What does this hiddenness look like in real life? Because Jesus embodied it perfectly, let's consider his life for guidance.

The Hidden Life of Jesus

Let this blow your mind: Jesus spent thirty of his thirty-three years on earth (about 90 percent of his life) in relative obscurity. As someone who regularly leads and speaks in front of lots of people, I find this so challenging. Ron Rolheiser explained how we can follow Jesus's example: "Ordinary life can be enough for us, but only if we first undergo the martyrdom of obscurity and enter Christ's hidden life."[1]

To value hiddenness doesn't mean we must become

members of a monastery, tucked away from the world. Rather, hiddenness is freedom from the shallow praise of the world.

In the Gospels, Jesus is constantly swarmed by admirers of his teaching and miracles, yet he refuses to capitalize on it. In modern terms, he doesn't post selfies (#LeperBe-Clean). On one occasion, when people are amazed at his miracles, here's how Jesus responds: "While he was in Jerusalem at the Passover Festival, many people saw the signs he was performing and believed in his name. But Jesus would not entrust himself to them" (John 2:23–24).

Even when people want to make him a celebrity, Jesus holds back. He's not wooed by platform. Even in his resurrection, Jesus prizes hiddenness. If it were me, I would show up at the home of those who crucified me to scare them to death and demonstrate my power over all things. Jesus, however, simply finds his friends and, rather than storming the world, tells them to share the good news.

To live this way is difficult, especially for those of us who use social media. It lures us into believing the primordial lie of the serpent: "You can be like God" (see Genesis 3:5). Social media creates the illusion that we can know all things, be everywhere, and use our words for the sake of power. It's the seductive lie that we can be omniscient, omnipresent, and omnipotent.

What's stunning about God's kingdom is that even though he *is* all-powerful, all-knowing, and everywhere-present, his presence and activity are often centered in places far from the masses:

In the fifteenth year of the reign of Tiberius Caesar—when Pontius Pilate was governor of Judea, Herod tetrarch of Galilee, his brother Philip tetrarch of Iturea and Traconitis, and Lysanias tetrarch of Abilene—during the high-priesthood of Annas and Caiaphas, the word of God came to John son of Zechariah in the wilderness. (Luke 3:1–2)

Luke lists all the political and religious leaders in power, then surprisingly highlights how the Word of God bypassed them and came to John in the wilderness. The locus of God's presence and activity is not found in the corridors of great power. The Gospels tell of a God who shows up in surprising places. His greatest place of action is hidden from the eyes of the socially powerful. His reach touches everything, but the center of it is hidden.

One of Jesus's best lessons on the importance of hiddenness is something he says about the Holy Spirit. It's easy to miss if you're not looking for it, so let's slow down and take a look.

Learning from the Holy Spirit

While wrapping up his time with his disciples before going to the cross, he utters this poignant line about the Holy Spirit: "When he, the Spirit of truth, comes, he will guide you into all the truth. He will not speak on his own; he will speak only what he hears, and he will tell you what is yet to come" (John 16:13). Eugene Peterson paraphrased Jesus's words, saying the Spirit "won't draw attention to himself" (MSG). That is why some people refer to him as the "Hidden Spirit."

The Holy Spirit shows deference to Jesus. His inclination is to spotlight another rather than hog the limelight, delighting in making the Son central. Jesus says, "He will glorify me because it is from me that he will receive what he will make known to you" (verse 14).

Within the Trinity, there is no jockeying for position. The three persons are radically other-focused. Just look at how their interaction is recorded in Scripture. The Father affirms the Son. "This is my Son, whom I love; with him I am well pleased. Listen to him!" (Matthew 17:5). The Son is always pointing to the Father. Jesus says things like, "The Father is greater than all. I do only what I see my Father doing." And the Spirit always points to the Son.

Here's the main idea: If the Spirit is secure in the love of the Trinity and if the Spirit lives inside you, he wants to make you secure too. He wants to remind you that you are loved by God. You are accepted by God. But ordering life around that theological truth requires concrete, counter-instinctual practices. What does it look like to live an anti-performance life? How does one get off the treadmill of posturing?

Practicing Hiddenness

I'll offer a few practices.

Hiddenness Is About Introspection, Not Introversion

It would be a mistake to correlate hiddenness with a personality trait. It is possible to be introverted while still wanting to be seen by others. Introversion is not a virtue; neither is extroversion. These personality traits are relational preferences that help us understand what gives us energy and what drains us. Depending on how we're wired, we might view introversion or extroversion as more "spiritual," but Christlikeness goes far deeper than personality preferences.

Hiddenness calls us to introspection—the examination of the interior of our lives. That's how we grow. As we pay attention to our motives, reactions, anxiety, and compulsions, we are given windows into our souls. At some point, we will be tempted to live for the praise and acknowledgment of others. As a public speaker, this temptation visits me regularly. I know I'm out of step with Jesus when I look to people to verify I'm enough. Of course, you need relationships that encourage and affirm the good you do, but there's a line that's crossed—a line only you can pinpoint—where instead of receiving encouragement, you're unhealthily chasing it.

As a public communicator, there are times when I want to stick around after my talk to bask in affirmation. On one occasion, after speaking at a large gathering, I felt that familiar urge to linger in people's compliments but had to run out immediately to catch a flight. As I drove to the airport, I felt disappointed that I missed all the words of encouragement and praise that would have been mine had I stayed around. After a few minutes, I realized God wanted me to practice hiddenness. Practicing introspection has not eliminated my desire for praise, but it does help keep it in check.

Hiddenness Requires Seasons of Absence

Beyond introspection, hiddenness is cultivated through seasons of absence. In the gospel stories, Jesus regularly withdraws, especially after fruitful ministry moments. Rhythms of hiddenness are necessary to protect him from the crowds. To be lured by the praise of the multitude exposes our souls to great danger. As Eugene Peterson said, "Church leaders frequently warn against the drugs and the sex, but, at least in America, almost never against the crowds."[2]

To practice hiddenness, then, requires seasons of Sabbath and fasting. In Sabbath, we are called to rest from our work. For many, the work we do is tied to our sense of self. To stop our work—even for a day—can call into question our identity and enoughness. To practice Sabbath is to intentionally orient one day out of seven around rest, not performance.

When it comes to fasting, I mostly have social media in mind. We are living on our electronic devices nonstop, seeking information and validation from others. One of the ways we demonstrate our freedom from something is by being willing to part from it. In my experiments with fasting from social media, I've learned an obvious but important principle: The less I post, the less I check. Conversely, the more I post, the more I check. When I remove apps from my phone for a day, a week, or a month (something I attempt to do each year at some point), I experience a spaciousness in my soul for God and those nearest to me. Unless we regularly withdraw, we will eventually wither.

Hiddenness Is Sustained by Prayer

It's no accident that in the same portion of the Sermon on the Mount where Jesus prescribes hiddenness, he also tells us to pray. Hiddenness, difficult as it may be, does *not* mean you are alone. Jesus says, "When you pray, go into your room, close the door and pray to your Father, who is unseen. Then your Father, who sees what is done in secret, will reward you" (Matthew 6:6).

In prayer, we are focused on communion with God, not currying favor with others. In silence, we root ourselves in the company of Father, Son, and Holy Spirit. In contemplation, we are invited into the holy sanctuary of God's embrace. Prayer wards off the unrelenting demands of our shadow side—that part of us that seeks to legitimize our existence through the rewards that come from the praise of people.

God Sees and Rewards

In giving ourselves to God in those three ways, Jesus pronounces the good news that we will be rewarded. We don't know what the reward will be—perhaps it will have something to do with the loving affirmation of the Father—but rest assured, Jesus sees you. Praise from others is temporary and ceasing; his reward is everlasting.

The Father sees the good you do in secret. If you take time to ponder all the goodness that has come your way, you'll realize it comes from a God who gives in secret. He delights in blessing you. When you choose to do the same, you become a bit more like God.

Interlude

PRAYER AND
THE NARROW PATH

Okay, before we get to Jesus's teachings on sex, money, worry, forgiveness, and more, let's take a quick breather lest you start despairing over how difficult these commands are. Everything in the Sermon on the Mount—everything in this book—is not telling you to try harder, muster will-power, or live a perfect life. You can't. I can't. What now?

Tucked into the middle of the Sermon on the Mount is the secret to walking Jesus's narrow path: prayer.

Prayer is both the entry point and the essential power that help us follow Jesus. To live like him requires us to pray like him. In other words, following Jesus is not just a matter of skill and grit; it is made possible through a life of being with God in prayer.

To follow Jesus and the way of his kingdom requires imitation. To live like him presupposes communion with him—a communion flowing out of an approach to prayer that engages the heart, captivates the mind, and directs the will.

Jesus's first disciples understood this.

In one story in the gospel of Luke, the disciples ask Jesus to teach them to pray (see Luke 11:1). This was a strange request because as young Jewish boys, they most certainly grew up praying. The average Jewish boy had entire books of the Old Testament memorized. Over the course of their lives, the disciples have prayed many prayers. They know the right words and have the correct cadence, but as they observe the life of Jesus, they realize that they aren't doing it right. Something is missing.

They have the words but not the fire.

They have Scripture memorized but not internalized.

They *know about* the God they worship, but Jesus seems to *truly know* the God of their ancestors.

They observe Jesus's joy, peace, power, and love, concluding he lives this way—in part—because of his prayer habits. So they ask him to take them to school.

I find it intriguing that the only recorded request of the disciples is connected to prayer. They never say, "Jesus, teach us to preach," or, "Teach us to cast out demons." Shockingly, they never ask him how to turn water to wine or multiply bread. (I would sign up for that messiah master class for sure.) Instead, they observe that the source of his life is communion with God.

Jesus hears their request and teaches them to pray. I want to highlight three important lessons in his prayer that will help us on the journey ahead.

First, following Jesus requires the empowerment of God. It requires dependence, not self-sufficiency. This is both a gift (we know we can't do it alone) and a challenge (we want to). The surprise of the Christian life is that the more we yield to God in prayer, the more God empowers us to live like Jesus. The church was birthed through the presence of the Holy Spirit. Christians are reborn through the work of the Holy Spirit. Christian formation is made possible only through the continual empowerment of the Spirit. To become like Jesus will always require us to be with God.

Second, prayer is not a list we bring to God but a practice that forms in us his love. It's common to view prayer as a strategy to get God to grant whatever we desire. Creating lists of requests tends to be the primary approach people take. And yes, there's a time for that. To bring our requests to God in prayer is a beautiful expression of humility, but when it's the *only* reason we pray, our relationship with him becomes transactional. Prayer is more about being *with* God than getting something *from* him—though he delights in blessing his children with good gifts. But prayer is about communion for the purpose of establishing communion with others. In short, prayer is about love.

Finally, prayer is about simplicity of heart and speech. Good news: You don't have to be a theologian or speak in Old English to pray! In fact, when Jesus teaches his disciples to pray, it's a prayer so simple that children can memorize it. Communion with God comes through simple speech, not flowery monologues. As we lift our minds and hearts to him in humble dependence, we receive the resources needed to walk the narrow path.

If we forget to commit our lives to prayer, the thought

of following Jesus's teachings will overwhelm and discourage us. Why? Because his teachings are not from this world. And teachings not from this world require an otherworldly power. That power is available to you every day.

So, with all that said, let's continue journeying together.

Part Two

WALKING THE NARROW PATH

4

OUR WITNESS

God sees more in us than we see in ourselves. Talk about good news, right? When we flip through the pages of the Holy Scriptures, time and time again we encounter flawed characters who don't seem to offer much—until they encounter God and, with his help, develop gifts and callings they never would have expected. I've been fortunate to experience this firsthand.

One of the reasons I mustered the courage to preach as a young nineteen-year-old is that God spoke to me through a group of preachers who saw something in me before I could see it myself. After a season of aimless wandering and anxiety, I surrendered my life to Jesus. I was overcome by his grace and felt an unshakable desire to proclaim the gospel to others. But I carried questions that made me hesitate: *Am I too young to preach? Do I need a degree first? Should I wait until I receive a ministry title? Does God want me to clean up all my struggles before I craft a sermon?* On and on the questions went. But within a short span of time, they were answered.

The small church I was attending in Brooklyn hosted worship gatherings for teenagers. Sometimes we visited other churches for their youth services. At these gatherings—much to my surprise—preachers I'd never met would affirm my call to pastoral ministry.

In the church tradition I was part of (Latino Pentecostal), space was usually created for the guest preacher to call people forward and speak a word of blessing or empowerment—an act of prophesying. That was all very new and strange to me.

The preacher said, "Young man in the blue shirt, please stand."

I looked down at my blue shirt and then around to make sure he wasn't talking about someone else. "Me?" I muttered with my index finger firmly pressed against my chest.

"Yes, you. Please stand."

In front of forty or fifty people, the preacher then said, "Young man, God has put a desire in your heart to preach. Pay attention to his voice stirring in your heart. You are called to proclaim the gospel."

I sat down, and the preacher moved on to the next teenager. This scene played itself out five times over the next six months. Different preachers in different churches essentially said the same thing: I was called to preach.

There's much that can be explored in this series of events, but what strikes me most is that I was a follower of Jesus for a very short time, yet God confirmed something that lived in me. In this next section of the Sermon on the Mount, that is exactly what Jesus does. He affirms our calling as his followers:

> You are the salt of the earth. But if the salt loses its saltiness, how can it be made salty again? It is no longer good for anything, except to be thrown out and trampled underfoot.
>
> You are the light of the world. A town built on a hill cannot be hidden. Neither do people light a lamp and put it under a bowl. Instead they put it on its stand, and it gives light to everyone in the house. In the same way, let your light shine before others, that they may see your good deeds and glorify your Father in heaven. (Matthew 5:13–16)

Jesus affirms his disciples. He recognizes their potential. He calls forth their power. He reveals to them their immense purpose. He calls them salt and light.

You Is Important

It's important to note that when Jesus uses the words *You are,* he's talking about the community. Naturally, we are called to be salt and light in our individual expressions of life, but primarily he has the church in mind. By the way, if Jesus was from New Jersey, he'd say, "*Yous guys are* the salt of the earth." If he was from the American South, he'd say, "*Y'all are* the salt of the earth."

In our life together as the church, we have a collective identity. This is important because from the beginning of the Bible to the end, we see that God is not interested in simply rescuing individuals; rather, he is forming a new community. A new family. A new humanity. The gospel is not just good news for our personal lives; it's the power of God to establish a new way of belonging to one another.

Here's the surprise: His disciples have just arrived. They are at the very start of their journey, but he doesn't say, "*You will be* salt and light when I'm done with you." He doesn't say, "*You have* salt and light." He doesn't say, "*You must* be salt and light."

He says, "*You are* salt and light."

Jesus calls out the very best in his disciples before they have demonstrated anything. And he does the same for you. You have much more to offer than you think because you are made in God's image, infused with gifts and purpose by the Creator.

It's easy to fixate on our gaps and failures, but Jesus looks at his followers and essentially says, "You have more to offer than you think because you are much more than you can imagine." Jesus aims his affirmation at disciples who are ordinary, unimpressive, and overlooked. His disciples are the religious version of the Bad News Bears. They don't have it all together.

In *The Help*, a movie about two black maids during the civil rights movement, there's a memorable scene in which the main character, Aibileen (a black maid and nanny), says to the child she cares for every day, "You is kind. You is smart. You is important."[1] Throughout the movie, the mother ignores and dismisses her child, yet every day, she hears those life-shaping words: "You is kind. You is smart. You is important."

At the start of the Sermon on the Mount, Jesus reinforces

the identity of his followers. To this small band of followers who live in the shadow of the mighty Roman Empire, Jesus reminds them of their great purpose in the world.

He looks into their eyes—and ours, too—and says, "You is salt. You is light. You is important." What does Jesus mean?

Salt of the Earth

In Jesus's day, salt was a very valuable commodity. In the surrounding Roman Empire, it played a significant role in commerce. In his book *Salt: A World History,* journalist Mark Kurlansky noted,

> The Roman army required salt for its soldiers and for its horses and livestock. At times soldiers were even paid in salt, which was the origin of the word *salary* and the expression "worth his salt" or "earning his salt." In fact, the Latin word *sal* became the French word *solde,* meaning pay, which is the origin of the word, soldier.[2]

Jesus uses this important metaphor to draw out at least two implications. First, salt *seasons.* It brings out the flavors in food, making it more enjoyable. As a Puerto Rican man with many years under my belt of eating properly seasoned food, when just the right amount of salt is added, it brings out the best in the meal.

When Jesus tells his followers they are salty, he's saying our very presence should draw out the best in others. The joy, peace, kindness, courage, compassion, and justice in our lives are meant to bring forth goodness all over the earth. Sadly, this has not always been the role Christians have embodied. Instead of adding flavor to others, we either under-season (distance ourselves from the world) or over-season (try to dominate the world). Too little salt and too much salt ruin a dish; the same applies to our relationship with the world.

Second, salt *sustains*. I think Jesus has this in mind as well. Long before we had refrigerators and freezers, salt was the main thing used to preserve food from decay and corruption. This is the assignment Jesus gives to you and me, as his disciples. We work for the preservation of the world. Wherever decay surfaces, Jesus calls us to be a preserving presence. We are to combat the decay of a broken world with the salt of our presence. Whether the decay is racism, poverty, gossip, relational dysfunction, or something else, Jesus calls us to preserve the good that exists.

Jesus sees so much potential in his disciples—in us—that he uses another metaphor to describe our witness in the world. He calls us the "light of the world" (Matthew 5:14).

Light of the World

Again, Jesus doesn't look to the future of his disciples and tell them what they could be. He announces good news from the start. They are already light. Jesus wants us to see ourselves the way he already does.

Some years ago, when I was just starting my preaching journey, I was invited to teach at a small, under-resourced church in the Bronx. After giving my message, I met with the pastor of the church in his office. He thanked me for my sermon, then said, "These folks are not the brightest crayons in the box." I was startled to hear him talk about his community that way. He saw his people as dim, despite their job description as kingdom luminaries—a title pronounced by Jesus himself. This dissonance between Jesus's words and his disturbed me.

The metaphor of light is a prominent theme in the Old Testament, particularly in the prophetic books. Isaiah said, "I will make you as a light for the nations, that my salvation may reach to the end of the earth" (Isaiah 49:6, ESV).

Jesus looks into the eyes of his ragtag community and says, "You are that light."

Of course, Jesus is *the* light. In John 8:12, he says, "I am the light of the world." But, remarkably, he gives his students the same title. In the same way the moon reflects the light of the sun, Jesus is *the* light, inviting his followers to reflect his brilliance in a dark world. Our light might not shine as bright, but he knows that a little bit of light goes a long way. Like salt, light has many purposes. One of its primary purposes is to scatter darkness.

Light helps us see. It makes things visible and reveals what would otherwise remain hidden. Light helps people find their way, especially to God. What a sacred calling!

Unfortunately, light can also be used to blind, not lead. When my children were young, they found a flashlight and made animal silhouettes on the wall with their hands. After a while, when that got boring, they started aiming the flashlight into each other's eyes. I realized very quickly that light can be wielded in harmful ways.

Sometimes it's easier for Christians to shine light on bad behavior—to highlight the vices in others—than shine light on our good Father. Many people believe that the gospel requires us to shine the spotlight on what's wrong with others. Shining a light is often a way to shame and condemn. However, that is not what Jesus means when he calls his followers *light*.

Warnings

Up until this point in the story, everything is going well. Jesus calls out the best in his novice disciples. He affirms who they are, but for each of these affirmations, he offers a warning about the temptation to neglect their call.

He says, "If salt has lost its taste, how shall its saltiness be restored? It is no longer good for anything except to be thrown out and trampled under people's feet" (Matthew 5:13, esv). In other words, don't lose your distinctiveness.

The greatest danger for Christians in every generation is being indistinguishable from the world. Will our values mirror the conventional wisdom of society, or will they confound it? Will we feign agreement on everything, or will we demonstrate love to those who see the world differently than we do? Will we define success based on net worth or on faithfulness to Jesus, no matter what the numbers say?

Jesus further warns his followers,

A town built on a hill cannot be hidden. Neither do people light a lamp and put it under a bowl. Instead they put it on its stand, and it gives light to everyone in the house. In the same way, let your light shine before others, that they may see your good deeds and glorify your Father in heaven. (verses 14–16)

He presents an intentionally unlikely scenario (lighting a lamp and putting it under a bowl), but it highlights the daily temptation to withhold and conceal the light. Let's consider two of the ways Christians posture themselves unhelpfully in relation to the world.

Apart from the World

Jesus expects us to be proximate to places of darkness. It's there we are called to shine our light. It is possible to possess the light of Jesus while remaining detached and disconnected from darkness, but what good does that do? In essence, we live *apart* from the world rather than *for* the world.

Beneath our distancing is usually fear. We don't want to be contaminated by the world. In some church traditions that emphasize personal holiness, being near those who don't share similar values is seen as a threat. Ironically, many of these traditions also carry a burden to bring others to faith in Christ. This frustrating dichotomy alienates the very people Jesus calls us to invite. Non-Christians become projects rather than friends. Look at Jesus, the *friend* of sinners.

During his earthly ministry, Jesus constantly moves closer to the people the religious leaders stand apart from: those with diseases or bad reputations, swindlers, the demon-possessed, and all types of sinners. In fact, that is the very nature of the Incarnation: to move toward us, in love. God moves into the neighborhood to dwell among us and dispel the darkness that overshadows us. Our job description—as light in a dark world—is to do the same.

Against the World

Another way to undermine our salt-and-light status is to live against the world. If living apart is rooted in fear of contamination, being against the world is rooted in fear of condemnation. In my first book, *The Deeply Formed Life*, I addressed this unhelpful posture:

> We are often known for what we are against rather than what we are for. A simple test will confirm this to be true. Bring up any divisive issue in our world— politics, sexuality, race, immigration, and so on—and what you'll find are Christians clearly asserting what they are against. But any conversation regarding the nature of God must begin with him being *for* all.[3]

Denouncing what we believe God is against is easy and spiritually lazy. While necessary, naming what is wrong is not the totality of being salt and light. To be against something is a great brand-builder. It's an effective political strategy. But it's a poor witness for Jesus. We are called to bring God's shalom into this world—to join our lives to him in service of others, offering them something of his life.

In his priestly prayer in John 17:15, Jesus says, "My prayer is not that you take them out of the world but that you protect them from the evil one." Jesus's narrow way doesn't have space for a life oriented around what it's against. There's nothing life-giving about that state of being. He calls us to presence and distinctness.

To be in the world but not of it requires a faith that is deeply present in the world but radically different from it.

Recapturing Our Mission

It's difficult for me to write a chapter on being salt and light without taking a moment to highlight the ways the church has not lived up to this holy calling. Christ followers have not always projected light. Instead of displaying the good life—defined by love, compassion, reconciliation, and peace—we simply mimic the world. It's easy to settle for being people who cast a shadow instead of shining brilliantly for God's kingdom.

The Quaker author and educator Parker Palmer captured this well in his book *Let Your Life Speak:* "A leader is someone with the power to project either shadow or light onto some part of the world and onto the lives of the people who dwell there. A leader shapes the ethos in which others must live, an ethos as light-filled as heaven or as shadowy as hell."[4]

Palmer had leaders in mind because of the enormous power they carry, but the same principle applies in our day-to-day lives. We project shadow or light. Sure, we have good and bad moments—we're all imperfect. But tracking the overall trend of our lives as Christians, which is it?

Glorifying the Father

Jesus calls us to concrete, observable acts of goodness. He calls us to let our light shine before others, in a way that glorifies God. Followers of Christ have one main objective: to display God's character. It might feel overwhelming and unattainable to think about displaying the character of the creator of the universe, but Jesus believes that it can be done through you.

I want you to think about the people you've avoided. The groups you've been against. The individuals you've written off. Yes, there are times to establish boundaries, and other times to stand against evil. But is your default posture one of being *against*? When you wake up in the morning, you choose to cast a shadow or light a candle. And from the very beginning of Jesus's sermon, he's calling you and me to reflect God's character. Why? Because the world longs to behold God. Humanity was created to live in his light. While sin darkens the world, there are traces of light that exist to point people to the True Light: We shine our lights not for ourselves but to glorify God. As we do, we will find ourselves journeying through the narrow but fulfilling way of his kingdom.

5

OUR ANGER

As I grew up in Brooklyn in the nineties, anger was essential for survival. I felt compelled to maintain a no-nonsense presence in the neighborhood just in case someone wanted to take advantage of me. It was a burdensome way of living. Eventually, this burden became something of an identity. Many young Brooklynites found pride in carrying anger. It was cool to carry rage. If you walked down the street with a Brooklyn bop (think of it as a stylish limp) and a scowl, it was proof you could handle yourself in the event of a spontaneous physical altercation. But this bop and scowl got me in trouble one time.

During one cold December in the mid-1990s, I was bopping down a block. The wool beanie I was wearing was low enough to almost cover my eyes. (In that age of style, the low beanie was another sign of toughness, at least in my neighborhood.) I looked across the street, thinking I saw a friend. (It didn't register with me at the time that I needed eyeglasses.) I looked in that direction for a solid five seconds, bopping away and squinting, when I realized that this wasn't a friend. Staring for five seconds with a low cap and exaggerated bop is an eternity. The guy I was looking at perceived my gaze as a threat and proceeded to run toward me. He blocked my path and asked if I was interested in a sparring match (not his words exactly). I reassured him I meant no harm in looking in his direction. He walked back to his house, and I bopped onward, relieved to avoid that altercation. In that moment, the prevalence of anger in my neighborhood was palpable.

When I became a Christian a few years after that moment, I was presented with a different understanding of anger. I was told anger is unbecoming for followers of Jesus and must be replaced with other Christian practices (you know, like denial). Instead of seeing anger as a means of survival—as I grew up thinking—it became something to suppress. Anger was a sign I was in "sinful flesh" (Romans 8:3). Apparently, angry people can't be in good relationship with God. I learned to quell my anger and call it "frustration."

For years, my wife, Rosie, would ask, "Are you angry?" I'd reply, "No, I'm just frustrated." She'd roll her eyes, knowing the truth about what I was feeling even though I was too ashamed to name it. I learned to deny my anger and called it discipline. I ignored it in the name of respectability. In the name of Jesus. I left no room for it and lied to others about my real feelings.

Anger is complicated because many of our families, cultures, and church communities have not made room for it whatsoever. How did your family do anger? How have the churches you've belonged to expressed anger? To what degree does your ethnic culture make room for anger? For many of us, it's suffocated out of our lives. When that happens, we are forced to live inhuman lives, leading to self-deception and emotional hiding. That was my story.

The question about anger is not whether or not we have it. The question is, to what level has it influenced our lives?

For years, I missed seeing the *gift* of anger. That may sound strange, but it's true. Anger is a gift—a way to appropriately respond to the incongruities and injustices of life. Anger is a way to release the valve of our souls when life surprises and wounds us. Anger, in the healthiest sense, identifies what needs to be made right. It's typically a secondary emotion—a symptom—of deeper angst. In all this, anger is not always the enemy. In Jesus's life, anger surfaces on a few occasions. Surprisingly, the first time is in the temple. Let me take you to that moment.

One day Jesus shows up at the temple. Knowing it's a place for worship and community, he is incensed to see the religious leaders exploiting the poor. He is having none of it. He fashions a whip, flips over the tables, and drives the leaders out.

Here's another example, which is the only time the word *anger* is directly tied to Jesus:

Another time Jesus went into the synagogue. A man with a weak and twisted hand was there. Some Pharisees were trying to find fault with Jesus. They watched him closely. They wanted to see if he would heal the man on the Sabbath day. Jesus spoke to the man with the weak and twisted hand. "Stand up in front of everyone," he said.

Then Jesus asked them, "What does the Law say we should do on the Sabbath day? Should we do good? Or should we do evil? Should we save life? Or should we kill?" But no one answered.

Jesus looked around at them in anger. He was very upset because their hearts were stubborn. Then he said to the man, "Stretch out your hand." He stretched it out, and his hand had become as good as new. (Mark 3:1–5, NIRV)

On both occasions—in the temple and the synagogue—Jesus's anger emerges because the poor and marginalized are being mistreated. Interestingly, he never responds this way when others mistreat *him*. It's always in defense of others.

Anger can sometimes be a redemptive gift when fueled by a desire to work for justice. In the words of theologian Barbara Holmes, "A theology of anger invites us to wake up from the hypnotic influences of unrelenting oppression so that individuals and communities can shake off the shackles of denial, resignation, and nihilism."[1]

Too often, though, anger is destructive, not redemptive, as Jesus plainly points out:

You have heard that it was said to the people long ago, "You shall not murder, and anyone who murders will be subject to judgment." But I tell you that anyone who is angry with a brother or sister will be subject to judgment. Again, anyone who says to a brother or sister, "Raca," is answerable to the court. And anyone who says, "You fool!" will be in danger of the fire of hell. (Matthew 5:21–22)

As I noted in a previous chapter, before Jesus talks about anger, he highlights the superficial righteousness of the Pharisees and how *his* disciples are to have a righteousness deeper than theirs. Some of the Pharisees meant well, but the collective spirit of this group was one of boundary making and spiritual pride. They set up many ways to determine who was in with God and who was out based on external behavior. Jesus effectively says, "In my kingdom, we don't just deal with the externals; we address the heart." Remember the beatitude "Blessed are the pure in *heart,* for they will see God." On the narrow path, true faithfulness comes from inner transformation. This is especially true as it relates to anger.

One could argue that the great sin of good religious people is anger. Think of the elder son in the parable of the prodigal son, who obeys his father his entire life but is resentful when his younger brother receives grace. To the legalist, grace is scandalous, not generous.

The religious leaders of the day thought they were spiritually healthy because they were not physically killing anyone. Not so! Jesus raises the bar. According to him, if you are angry with your brother or sister, you are subject to judgment.

The anger Jesus names is very specific. In Greek, it's *orgizomenos.* Biblical scholar Dale Bruner noted this is a present-tense word that can be best translated, "is carrying anger," "is remaining angry," or "is nursing a grudge."[2] Jesus isn't criticizing a single moment of anger. He doesn't say, "Whoever gets angry." Instead, he warns us about carrying it, nursing it, remaining in it. American philosopher Dallas Willard helpfully described a life suspended in perpetual bitterness: "Energy is dedicated to keeping the anger alive: we constantly remind ourselves of how wrongly we have been treated."[3]

When rage becomes the default mode of our lives, sooner or later it weighs us down. Have you ever been at the supermarket when it seems like everyone on the planet has the same idea? You can't find a grocery cart, so you settle for one of those handbaskets. Little by little, the basket gets filled. As you walk from aisle to aisle, the weight of the items—almost imperceptibly—makes one of your arms hang down. Pretty soon the basket feels too heavy to carry. When it comes to anger and resentment—aka, *orgizomenos*—many of us are like that basket: frustrated, stockpiling anger, slowly getting weighed down. Bruner aptly commented, "He is a fool who cannot *be* angry; but he is wise who will not *remain* so."[4]

How do you know if you're harboring unhealthy anger? Jesus gives two examples, the first of which is the word *raca*.

Raca is not a word we use today, but there are plenty of similar words that flow from our lips. *Raca* can be translated "fool," "idiot," or "jerk" (words I hear often on Queens Boulevard while driving). What makes a word problematic—even dangerous—is the spirit of contempt animating it. *Raca* is a dehumanizing word. It's a word of condemnation. It's a word intended to cause great harm, even when muttered casually on our Tuesday commute. To get to the seriousness of the word, it's like saying the N-word to a black man or woman—a term I heard for the first time in my midtwenties.

Here's what happened. I was on a trip with a few other young adults from my local church. We were going to spend a few days leading worship and preaching at a wealthy Christian high school. That week, I stayed with a kind family who had two teenage sons. One morning, one of the sons drove me to the school. His friend sat in front while I sat in back. As we came to a red light, there was a black man, who seemed to be homeless, walking down the street. The friend in the front seat proceeded to lower his window and yell—in the most dehumanizing voice—"Get out of this neighborhood, N-word." But he didn't say, "N-word"; he actually used the word that is easily regarded as one of the most despicable words one can utter. I sat in the back seat stunned and, to my shame, did not confront the teenager on the spot. I was caught off guard, having never heard that word, not to mention how it was spoken in such a demonizing spirit. That's *raca*. If you haven't noticed, we live in a *raca* world.

In our society, anger is nurtured and rewarded. We are formed to see others as the root problems of society, justifying our anger toward them.

Democrat? *Raca*.

Republican? *Raca*.

Immigrant? *Raca*.

Gay person? *Raca*.

Pro-life person? *Raca*.

Atheist? *Raca*.

Baptist? *Raca*.

On and on it goes. Here's Jesus's point: To carry and nurse the kind of anger that leads to *raca* is murder in God's eyes. You don't have to spill blood to kill life. To speak a mean-spirited, dehumanizing word subjects us to judgment and the power of hell. If you've ever experienced that level of hatred toward someone, while it can feel justified in the moment, you're actually living in a kind of hell. Rage consumes us. Destroys us. Still, we don't see the damage done to our lives. It's hard not to think Jesus is exaggerating just a bit. In fact, it's easy to deceive ourselves into thinking anger is a fruit of the Spirit. Beware of whitewashing toxic anger with slick names like "righteous indignation," "standing up for truth," or "telling it like it is." If Jesus says it's destructive, we must make every effort to rid our lives of it.

Cultural and Interior Anger

When I read Jesus's words in Matthew 5, I wonder, *How does someone become filled with harmful anger? Is it just a personality flaw? A bad habit? Biological or neurological?* The blowups we see in domestic violence, road rage, angry outbursts at our children, self-hatred, or simmering contempt don't come out of nowhere. I see two sources: our culture and our interior. Let's briefly unpack both.

Cultural Anger

A study was done in 2021 highlighting a truth about social media that many people have observed: When tweets and posts are fueled by moral outrage, they receive more "likes" and "retweets."[5] This amplification—which rewards anger in the form of dopamine and new followers—creates a vicious cycle. Outrage becomes a way to build a brand or social identity. In some cases, there is money to be made as well. In our attempt to locate the problems of our world outside ourselves, individuals or entire groups of people become the objects of our wrath. We stand outside of any critique, pointing our index finger outward. Few things fuel anger like self-righteousness. Here's a tough but important question: Can you recognize ways you point a finger while ignoring your own shortcomings, or are you living in a fantasy in which you're always right?

Interior Anger

Going one level deeper than cultural anger, let's examine interior anger. It is emotionally satisfying (at least momentarily) to transmit our anger rather than face it. To be angry is to feel in control. It's a convenient way to distance ourselves from weakness and vulnerability. It's a way to give the illusion of strength. When anger bubbles up from within, it's usually because of unmet expectations, anxiety, or the need to be in charge.

Whether we realize it or not, internally there is always a story we're telling ourselves in the moment. I'll never forget the time I was interviewed on the topic of "being a calm presence." An hour before my interview, I severely strained my voice. No, I hadn't been at a sporting event; it was from screaming at my eight-year-old son in the car as I dropped him off during the first week of school. As we approached the school building that morning, he started crying uncontrollably. He would later tell me that he was afraid of playing outdoors during recess because of his fear of being stung by a bee (something that happened before). He didn't have the ability to self-regulate and share his deep-seated fear. His refusal to go to school made me late for the podcast interview. Instead of telling my interviewer that I had a situation to take care of, I did the next "best" thing: I yelled as loud as I could, trying to threaten my son to go to school. Turns out that my moment of temporary insanity stung him worse than any bee could and left me ashamed.

The story in my head was around being responsible and prompt, but it was more so about the powerless feeling I had around meeting my son compassionately in his distress.

I realized that compassionate and curious introspection was required of me after that moment, especially if I was going to be the father my son needs me to be. You see, it takes more than willpower to appropriately manage the anger within.

Resisting Anger

In his sermon, Jesus doesn't offer a bulleted list of practices to put anger in its proper place. (Nothing wrong with that—in the next section, I'll offer a spiritual practice for helping us handle our anger.) Instead, he offers us a staggering image that shows how to manage anger and also how to be in right relationship with God.

Jesus says that your relationship with God is not as good as you think if your relationship with another person is damaged. There is no way to truly commune with God if you harbor *orgizomenos* toward your neighbor. What's more, Jesus counsels his followers to delay worship until immediate attention is given to the estrangement.

He imagines a worshipper about to bring a sacrifice for one's sins (a standard practice in ancient times). It was often the case that worshippers would travel long distances to Jerusalem to perform these rituals. This is where Jesus surprises us. If someone is about to offer a sacrifice but remembers an unresolved issue with someone, they should stop at once. They should go back home, find the person they disagree with, try to reconcile, and *then* come back and finish the sacrifice. Here's his point: We can't be in relationship with the Lord of life if we are secretly harboring death in our hearts.

Additionally, Jesus's instructions speak to the urgency of the moment. It doesn't take much for a little bit of anger to grow into consuming rage. He is teaching us to guard our hearts against a power that seeks to destroy us—and our neighbor. He knows that left untended, anger leads us to internalize messages about ourselves and others, making it permissible to destroy people in our hearts, with our words, and through our actions. He prods us to get *beneath* the surface of our anger to make room for God's power. How do we do this? I recommend a spiritual practice called *lament*.

Practicing Lament

There are legitimate reasons to be angry. But in the kingdom of God, there's no legitimate reason to let that anger destroy and consume you. I've found that the practice of lament—voicing my pain, grief, and distress to God—helps me defuse my anger.

Anger closes us in; lament opens us up. Rather than ignoring an offense, lament creates space in our hearts for God's Spirit to redirect our hearts and get to the root of the anger. It may surprise you that the root of rage is often grief. That is why slowing down to lament must be part of our regular worship gatherings and our interactions with trusted friends. Paired with lament, our anger can be a catalyst for opening us up to God's life, love, and power. Unless we face our anger honestly (and in the presence of God), we violate the law of love—the law that matters most to Jesus.

Paul's command to the church at Ephesus is helpful here: "Be angry and do not sin; do not let the sun go down on your anger, and give no opportunity to the devil" (Ephesians 4:26–27, ESV). In other words, allow yourself to experience anger, but be mindful of its power to enslave you to a larger evil force. Or in the well-known words of James, "Everyone should be quick to listen, slow to speak and slow to become angry" (James 1:19).

Slow to Anger

The good news of the gospel is this: God himself is "slow to anger and abounding in steadfast love" (Psalm 145:8, ESV). In the Old Testament, this phrase is repeated numerous times, pointing to a central characteristic of God. While it is common to view him as capricious and vengeful, his patience is one of the most staggering qualities about him.

Just take a look at the repeated failures, rebellion, and stubbornness of the people of God. From one moment to the next, they switch loyalties, surrender their calling, and run after other gods. Yet God's anger travels in slow motion, giving his people multiple opportunities to change direction. When you think about your life, do you see your story in theirs? Like the anger of the father in the parable of the prodigal son, God's anger unfolds in slow motion but his steadfast love moves to us with hyper-speed. How comforting this is!

The God revealed in Jesus Christ does not store up anger

against us. He does not mutter the word *raca* under his breath. Rather, Christ is the one who received the *raca* of the world in its fullness and, in turn, pours out forgiveness and mercy.

To show up in the world as a follower of Jesus, then, is not to eliminate all forms of anger but to live in such a way that it doesn't consume you. You are human, so you *will* get angry. But with Christ's love compelling you, and his Spirit transforming you, anger won't own you. On the narrow path, hemmed in by grace on all sides, you will find freedom from rage and know satisfaction that lasts.

6

OUR WORDS

"Did you leave work yet?" I see my wife's text, knowing I told her I'd be home at a certain time. I type a quick reply: "Oh yeah, honey. I left twenty minutes ago." Meanwhile, I frantically throw my laptop and books in my bag and sprint out of the office.

Every day—in big and seemingly small ways—it's tempting to compromise the truth. When someone invites me to an event and I'm not really interested in going, my capacity for lying surfaces effortlessly. Instead of plainly saying, "I'm sorry, but I can't make it," on occasion I've made up events to justify my absence.

When a friend asks if I received their text, rather than admit I did and need to think about the question he asked, I'm dishonest at times: "No, I didn't get it. Can you send it again?"

In a world immersed in lies, telling the truth is a revolutionary act. On any given day, we are confronted with the question, *Will I tell the truth or will I lie?* This elementary question has all kinds of applications. Whether on the playground, in the boardroom, or on social media, integrity is not our default. It's not like we wake up in the morning intending to deceive, but it's nonetheless easy to drift into dishonesty.

The issue of lying has pervaded our world from the very beginning. In modern life, with the nonstop flow of information and news, we are exposed to lying in every arena of life—including the church. Lies spoken by pastors, religious leaders, and denominations dominate the headlines. Leaders in the highest levels of government perpetuate propaganda: half truths packaged as whole truths. CEOs and leaders of powerful institutions cover up dishonesty, leveraging power to preserve their brands.

Most lies, however, never make the big stage. These are the "little" lies spoken at work, at home, and in our hearts. We lie about our true feelings on a matter. We lie to cover up our weaknesses. We lie to gain some kind of advantage in our careers. The list goes on.

When you believe (or tell) a lie, you are not free. God created you for freedom—to enjoy the benefits of truthfulness, honesty, and integrity. The degree to which we live in truth is the degree to which we live in the way of Jesus. As we'll see in this section of the Sermon on the Mount, the narrow path is a place where plain, honest speech is the standard:

You have heard that it was said to the people long ago, "Do not break your oath, but fulfill to the Lord the vows you have made." But I tell you, do not swear an oath at all: either by heaven, for it is God's throne; or by the earth, for it is his footstool; or by Jerusalem, for it is the city of the Great King. And do not swear by your head, for you cannot make even one hair white or black. All you need to say is simply "Yes" or "No"; anything beyond this comes from the evil one. (Matthew 5:33–37)

Oaths, Promises, and Integrity

Jesus is referencing a common ancient practice: Oaths were essentially a way to add oomph to a promise. In an oral society, where written contracts weren't a cultural norm like today, one's word was legally binding. So far, so good. Jesus is not looking to reject the Old Testament's value on making oaths so much as he is exposing the deceptive ways the practice was carried out. The people in Jesus's day figured out a way to manipulate the truth while still appearing upright.

Here's how it worked: If you made a promise by invoking God's name, there was no way to get out of the promise. But what if you could insert religious language not as weighty as God's name but still profound enough to bolster your promise? That is the loophole Jesus critiques. Rather than swearing on God's name, they would swear by the holy city or the sacred temple. Somewhere along the way, their yes became no. Their commitment was nullified, their promise invalid.

When I was in elementary school, I'd routinely get into some conflict with a friend or relative. If I broke a cousin's toy by accident and didn't want to admit my crime, I'd make a dramatic statement to prove my innocence. The conversation went like this:

"Did you break my toy?"

"No, I didn't."

"But you were the only one here."

"I swear to you I didn't. I swear on my mother's grave."

"Oh, okay, I believe you."

Simple as that. At that age, we believed that padding the truth with a phrase like "on my mother's grave" confirmed one's honesty. Of course, I'd have my fingers crossed behind my back to avoid God's judgment. (One can never be too careful.)

Many children seem to have an implicit understanding that our word is our bond. I recall a day when my five-year-old daughter asked me to take her to get ice cream after dinner. Without looking at my calendar, I said, "Sure, honey." I realized afterward that I had an evening meeting that couldn't be rescheduled. When dessert time came, she asked for the ice cream. I nonchalantly told her that I forgot about a meeting and that we would get some the next day. Her response? With tears in her eyes, she uttered the three words that kids all over the world have stored deep in their souls: "But you promised!"

My quick response was, "Darling, I never promised you that." And you already know how the rest of the conversation went.

What happened? She understood my plain word to be a sure promise. Jesus knows it's not just children who are affected by this lack of promise keeping and truthfulness. Without truthfulness, the very fabric of society tears apart.

Jesus offers a radical shift in perspective for those who want to follow him. He calls us to the kind of integrity that prioritizes truthfulness, especially when it comes to keeping our promises. Before we unpack this, it's important to name why we have trouble with this concept. Why aren't we truthful? Why do we say yes when we mean no? Why don't we fulfill our commitments? Why is there often a chasm between what we say and what we do?

Untruthfulness

When I think about my own life—as a pastor and a recovering people pleaser—I can name three reasons why I've been untruthful: fear of disappointing others, living life on the go, and being immersed in a culture of superficiality.

Fear of Disappointing Others

To tell the truth is to risk disappointing others. Many of us are constantly conforming to what we believe is expected of us, especially by people we hold in high regard. We don't want to offend, as theologian Stanley Hauerwas noted,

> I think we lie often not because we're liars, but because we're moderately good people who don't want to hurt anyone, and therefore we often times restrain ourselves from saying what needs to be said, because we don't want to live with the results.[1]

One of my ongoing areas for growth is being truthful with Rosie, even as we approach two decades of marriage. There have been many times in our relationship when I had a difference of opinion on a matter—whether it was vacation plans, financial priorities, or an approach to parenting.

It took years before I had the courage to simply state my opinion on the matter. What generated this hesitancy? Fear of disappointing and hurting her. But I've come to understand that I'm not doing her (or our relationship) any favors by avoiding my perspective. Even more, falsely, my silence communicated that she couldn't handle my honesty. In actuality, it's *me* who can't handle disagreement.

We lie because we long to be loved. There's something in each of us that desires affection and belonging. When this isn't felt, we create paths to secure it. Alarmingly, lying achieves this for us (partially). I've had numerous conversations with congregants who want so badly to be loved by a particular person or group that they fail to set healthy limits on their time and energy.

I remember meeting Jerry (not his real name) at a volunteer event. In my short conversation with him, I noted how grateful I was for his sacrificial service to our church (a pastor's dream). A few weeks later, we sat down for breakfast and I began to ask some general questions about the state of his marriage. I realized he was overextending himself by serving the church, to the point that his health and marriage were suffering. His body was saying no but his mouth kept saying yes. When I asked about his inability to practice Sabbath keeping and cultivate healthy rhythms of connection with his wife, his motivations surfaced.

"Pastor Rich," he said hesitantly, "I'm afraid if I say no or limit my service to the church, I won't receive attention and praise from many in our congregation for the work I do as a leader."

In that moment, I had to confess my own familiarity with this temptation. If we base our identities on being loved and esteemed, eventually it will crush us—from the constant effort it takes to please others and because we'll never be able to keep people happy forever.

Living Life on the Go

Why do we fail to keep commitments? It's often because the pace at which we live is not sustainable for the decisions we make. Let me rephrase this in emotionally healthy language: The pace at which *I* live is often not sustainable for the decisions *I* make. I know what it's like to overcommit myself to numerous projects. I know what it's like to say yes because I was trying to be helpful, which created an avalanche of yeses that led to exhaustion and family tension.

Many of us idolize busyness; it makes us feel important. We get sucked into a vortex of activity—especially "good" activity because our sense of self is validated. But that leads to a problem: There's no margin for stepping back, discerning what's best, or resting.

Because I've committed myself to so many things over the years, my new habit is to let people know I will think about a given invitation before agreeing to it. If I find it difficult to reflect on whether I can truly commit to something, it is a sign I should say no. I'm a work in progress here, but I've released many burdens through this practice.

Creating margin for internal clarity is necessary for truthfulness. When we discover and articulate our values, we are free from the entanglements of what we think others want from us. I once talked with a friend who was so clear about his vocation as a pastor that his immediate no to an invitation surprised me. I had asked if he would consider joining our congregation in a pastoral role. I was sure he would ask for time to pray about the idea. (And by the way, saying, "Let me pray about it," has often been my strategy to avoid giving a clear no in the moment.) Instead, without missing a beat, he said, "No, I'm not called to leave my congregation. I'm there to stay." I admired his clarity of heart and simple words. There was no pretense. He slowed down his life enough to let his no be no. You can have that same kind of clarity, but first you'll have to slow down, consider your priorities, and then graciously but relentlessly protect them.

Culture of Superficiality

Finally, untruthfulness surfaces because we often find ourselves swimming in a shallow culture where people are rarely honest. When asked, "How are you?" the automatic response is, "Blessed! Not stressed!" In some environments—especially Christian circles—honesty and truth-telling feel too risky. Sadly, our vision of discipleship leaves no room for bad days. In the church, it's common to see mental health conditions such as depression as a sin. It's also common to assign moral judgment to seasons of pain. And, of course, many don't feel safe disclosing intimate parts of their lives to people who don't offer a loving presence. This is tragic: Communities that foster untruth are not sustainable or life-giving.

Take a moment to reflect on these three challenges before us. How has your fear of disappointing people made you dishonest? How has life on the go hurt your ability to offer a yes or no from a centered place? How has a culture of superficiality contaminated your integrity? As we follow Jesus closely, we are given a new place to live from. As you slow your life down to be with him, your words will come from a stable place. As you live in his love, you will grow in honesty about how you are really doing.

All this is important because of what lying does to us.

What Comes from the Evil One

When we lie consistently, it eventually becomes our reality. And when that happens, our souls are in grave danger.

There's a contested saying of Jesus regarding blaspheming the Holy Spirit that gets at this. I'll summarize the story found in Matthew 12:22–37.

At this point in Jesus's ministry, he consistently demonstrates his authority over demons. When a demon-possessed person comes near him, it doesn't take long for that person to be delivered. Jesus is doing meaningful ministry for the community, but the religious establishment feels threatened by his existence. His presence jeopardizes their power. No matter how much good Jesus does, it clashes with their self-serving narrative. Despite the power and beauty of his healing ministry, they couldn't see, savor, or receive it.

In that day, for someone to cast a demon out of a person proved God's favor on that person's life, yet these religious leaders persist in claiming that Jesus isn't from God. No one can deny the miracles Jesus is doing, so they accuse him of partnering with Satan. They insist that he's operating out of demonic power. In response, Jesus issues this sober warning: "Anyone who speaks a word against the Son of Man will be forgiven, but anyone who speaks against the Holy Spirit will not be forgiven, either in this age or in the age to come" (verse 32).

How should we understand this warning? Ron Rolheiser summarized it well:

> Be careful about what you are doing just now, putting a false spin on something because it is too awkward to accept as true. The danger is that if you continue doing this you may eventually come to believe your own lie. That will be unforgivable, given that you will no longer want to be forgiven because you will see truth as a lie and a lie as the truth.[2]

Lying is not just a sign of questionable character; it's captivity to an evil power. And this evil can be driven out only by speaking the truth.

Speaking the Truth

What does speaking the truth look like? Here are a few thoughts.

First, it means we say what we mean. I remember a moment when I was very defensive toward Rosie when she pointed out a blind spot of mine. Her words exposed an area of growth I needed to give my attention to. But instead of humbly listening, I verbally lashed out at her. A few moments later, having realized the error of my ways, I asked her, "Honey, can you forgive me?" Her response surprised me, but I appreciated her honesty. She said, "Eventually I will." Because of our relationship, I knew that her hesitation didn't mean the end of our marriage; it simply meant she wouldn't say something she didn't mean.

Second, speaking truthfully means we do what we say. Being truthful is ultimately about alignment; it's a matter of congruence. What's happening on the outside is consistent with what's going on inside. To speak truth is to, by God's grace, follow through. A life of integrity narrows the gap between the words we say and the way we live.

Third, speaking truthfully means that whatever we speak in one place is what we speak everywhere else. Do you ever express an opinion to one person, then adjust your level of conviction with another? Why do we feel the need to change our views? What is it about a certain person that makes you repackage your perspective? To live with integrity, you can't shape-shift to meet the expectations of whomever you're with.

Finally, speaking the truth in the way of Jesus requires the presence of love. It is common for truth-telling to be cut off from love. In fact, speaking the truth without love has become a sign of authenticity. As Dietrich Bonhoeffer said, "Truth just for oneself, truth spoken in enmity and hate is not truth but a lie, for truth brings us into God's presence, and God is love. Truth is either the clarity of love, or it is nothing."[3] To be sure, this doesn't mean that our words will always sound nice and polished. But it does mean that love is what animates the truth we seek to offer.

Promise Making and Promise Keeping

As a pastor, I have a front-row seat to the multitude of commitments people—including me—make. To be part of a community means that we will have various opportunities to commit our time, energy, and gifts in service to others. But this clashes with a culture that seeks to be free from all kinds of obligation. *Obligation* is a dirty word for many people. It connotes responsibility without corresponding desire. It sounds like coercion, not generosity. It doesn't *feel* good. But following Jesus doesn't always *feel* good. In fact, he calls his followers to take up their crosses and follow him (see Matthew 16:24–25).

Promising to do something for another is a beautiful reflection of the kingdom of Jesus. When two people get married, they promise to be for each other through all stages of life. In so doing, they image the covenantal love of God toward his people. (I'm fully aware that Jesus makes provision for us to set aside the vows we make in the presence of relational violations such as adultery. This teaching needs to be nuanced in such a way that people are not unduly forced to remain in a harmful relationship.)

When I became the lead pastor of New Life Fellowship, we had a transition ceremony. My predecessor stood in front of me in the presence of our congregation and invited me to promise that I would carry out my duties faithfully by the grace of God. When I made that promise, I felt the weightiness of my calling and the ways I was reflecting God's shepherding heart to this flock. There's something powerful about honoring our promises for one another. My life is richer because of the commitments I've made and kept, and though it's hard to follow through sometimes, God honors those who pursue integrity (albeit imperfectly).

God's Yes Is Yes

There is no vacillation in God. He says what he means and keeps his promises. What does this tell us? Minimally, that we can trust God's character. In Christ, God has demonstrated his irrevocable commitment toward humanity. He promises to be for us, pledging his presence and steadfast love. We don't have to worry whether he will love us today and change his mind tomorrow. No, that has been settled. You can bank on God's care for you.

Maybe you've lived through some hard times. Life hasn't been easy, and as a result, you question whether God will *actually* keep his promises. Maybe you doubt his faithfulness toward you. Perhaps a recent setback has disoriented you completely. Maybe broken promises from well-meaning people have tainted your view of God. I can't know everything you've been through, but I want to remind you that all God's promises are "Yes and amen" in Christ Jesus. His Word is faithful. His promises are trustworthy.

As you follow Jesus down the narrow path, you will see his faithfulness in your life. Slowly but surely, he will transform you into someone whose words are trustworthy and intentional.

7

OUR DESIRES

I remember the morning of May 19, 2018, well. I was sound asleep, when out of nowhere, a bright light entered the room. I started to hear festive music and singing. For a moment, I thought I was at the gates of heaven. It turns out that Rosie had turned on the television at 5:00 A.M. to watch the royal wedding of Prince Harry and Meghan Markle. My wife was not the only one tuning in that day.

There were twenty-nine million people who watched it. Why was so much attention given to this couple? Certainly, many have a fascination with all things related to the crown, but I think there's a deeper answer. I remember reading the words of a nun named Miriam James. She tweeted,

Why does the human heart love a good #RoyalWedding? Because our deepest desire is to be presented pure, holy, and spotless before the One who will eternally love us in unending, intimate communion.[1]

If that's not a nun mic drop, I don't know what is! Whether married or single, we regularly need a vision of marriage as an icon of God's passionate love for the world. Of all the topics Jesus covers in the Sermon on the Mount, his words on adultery and lust arguably produce the most resistance.

As a pastor, after teaching on those topics, I've received emails saying something like, "We should not preoccupy ourselves with what people do in the privacy of their homes." I've been in small groups where someone gently expresses a view of human sexuality that depicts the Bible as "culturally conditioned" and therefore "requires a new lens of interpretation." My heart is with them, as there are many ways the church talks about sexuality that are unkind and unhelpful.

Jesus does not neatly resolve all the questions we hold pertaining to sexual ethics, but he *is* clear that God cares deeply about the desires and how we steward them. What we do with our sexual desires is connected to our relationship with him. I know how narrow that can sound, but Jesus is ushering us onto a beautiful part of the narrow path where instead of using one another in lust, we love one another with purity and kindness. Inside all of us, we desire this kind of life—one that is free, faithful, and fruitful. Sadly, our world commodifies sex in a way that exploits and objectifies others, which is why—as we're about to see—Jesus rails against the sexual ethic of his day (and ours as well).

The Destructive Force of Lust

As usual, not only is Jesus concerned with behavior, but he gets to the root of the problem. In an ancient culture that frowns upon adultery, he knows that someone can technically never cheat while harboring all sorts of lust in their heart and mind. By making adultery an internal sin, not just an external one, he speaks to everyone who nurtures lust, whether single or married:

> You have heard that it was said, "You shall not commit adultery." But I tell you that anyone who looks at a woman lustfully has already committed adultery with her in his heart. (Matthew 5:27–28)

In our pornified smartphone age, Jesus equates lustful gazing with adultery! Who hasn't indulged in that kind of gazing nowadays? As if that isn't intense enough, Jesus takes it to another level:

> If your right eye causes you to stumble, gouge it out and throw it away. It is better for you to lose one part of your body than for your whole body to be thrown into hell. And if your right hand causes you to stumble, cut it off and throw it away. It is better for you to lose one part of your body than for your whole body to go into hell. (verses 29–30)

Adultery is betrayal, arguably the deepest kind. When two people make vows to each other before God and a community, they pledge to love the other through the ups and downs of life. Within Christian marriages, we get married not just *in* a church but *for* the church. In other words, our love is on display for all to see, pointing people to God's passionate commitment for the church and the world at large.

Jesus names all this but then takes it further. He presents the narrow way of resisting adultery of the heart. He calls us to confront our lust.

Jesus knows that most people—then and now—would say, *I've kept that commandment. I haven't committed adultery. I haven't slept with someone outside my marriage.* Or if we are not married, we simply skip this part altogether. But not so fast. Jesus reminds us again that belonging to him and to live in his kingdom means our desires, our thoughts, and our intentions must be shaped by his love.

In the Sermon on the Mount, the concept of lust is similar to anger: Both can be silently nursed into the heart, corrupting the soul, even if they don't explode into full-blown adultery or murder. When Jesus says, "Whoever lusts," he's not referring to a passing attraction; he means intentionally nursing an illicit fantasy. As long as lust is present, love cannot be.

Lust is about consumption. Love is about communion.

Lust is about taking. Love is about giving.

Lust uses. Love honors.

Lust diminishes the other. Love cherishes the other.

We were created by God to enjoy communion with one another. We were created by God to have relationships characterized by dignity and respect. Tragically, we live in a society where consuming others for our own enjoyment is the norm. Thus, we are shaped to fulfill our desires however and whenever we want. We are formed to believe relationships are just a means to a sexually satisfying end.

That is a very prevalent and dangerous reality in our day. Due to the impact of pornography in our culture, we are formed to create imaginary relationships that negatively affect our ability to genuinely connect with others. Just look at these overwhelming statistics:

- Porn sites receive more monthly traffic than Netflix, Amazon, and Twitter combined.[2]

- 35 percent of all internet downloads are porn-related.[3]

- 34 percent of internet users have been exposed to unwanted porn via ads or pop-ups.[4]

- At least "30 percent of all data transferred across the Internet is porn."[5]

According to one study, "teens and young adults rank not recycling as more immoral than viewing porn."[6] And the problem gets even more complicated as technology advances.

In the *Journal of Sexual and Relationship Therapy*, researchers in Canada predicted we are heading for a day (and we might already be there) when "some will prefer to have loving relationships with sex robots instead of humans."[7] Dr. Neil McArthur, professor of philosophy and director of the Centre for Professional and Applied Ethics at the University of Manitoba, wrote,

It is safe to say the era of immersive virtual sex has arrived. . . .

As these technologies advance, their adoption will grow and many people will come to identify themselves as "digisexuals"—people whose primary sexual identity comes through the use of technology.

Many people will find that their experiences with this technology become integral to their sexual identity and some will prefer them to direct sexual interactions with humans.[8]

These technological developments reveal that, increasingly, culture sees sex more as a commodity to consume than as an invitation to love another human well. That distinction—between consumption and communion—is crucial for understanding Jesus's narrow path.

Consumption Versus Communion

Our world today is different than in Jesus's ancient context, but the same human impulse remains: the temptation to use others. Whenever consumption replaces communion, our souls are corrupted.

Although objectifying others is a temptation for all people, when reading this portion of Jesus's sermon, I can't help but notice how he challenges men in particular. This is expected: In his ministry, he regular confronts the male-dominated society he lives in. He receives women to be his disciples—a social and religious taboo in his time. He speaks to a Samaritan woman by a well (also socially unacceptable). Jesus regularly empowers and affirms the dignity of women.

For thousands of years, women have been seen as objects and property for men's satisfaction. Women have been blamed for male lust. The Pharisees of Jesus's day believed that the key to eliminating male lust was for men to *avoid all contact with women*. Rather than take responsibility for their own actions, these religious leaders assumed women were the primary problem. Jesus rejects this line of thinking and calls us to take ownership of what flows from our hearts.

According to Jesus, the primary way to deal with lust is not "out there"; it's "in here"—that is, in our hearts. In some evangelical spaces, it's common to create boundaries around sexual integrity but in a way that makes women seem dangerous or untrustworthy. The Billy Graham rule is a well-known example. To protect himself from false accusations, he would avoid all one-on-one situations with women, even a brief trip on an elevator. While boundaries are important to maintain, they sometimes place women in a morally inferior position. Jesus names this and puts the onus on the man's heart. Men, the way to avoid sexual impropriety is to deal with our own lust. I remember taking my annual mandatory staff training on anti–sexual harassment. One of the slides read,

> Men: Do not avoid working with women because you're afraid of sexual-harassment complaints. To avoid sexual harassment complaints, do not sexually harass people.

Exactly.

Now, I want to note that just because Jesus speaks to men here, it doesn't mean women are not in danger of lusting. He speaks to men primarily but not exclusively. There are plenty of ways women are tempted by the power of lust. Remember, the sin of lust is about creating relationships in your head for sexual gratification.

Temptations like watching pornography or reading fantasy novels are ever-present in today's world. If a woman sees a man as simply an object to meet her emotional or physical desires, she is in danger as well.

The question is not *if* we will encounter lust but rather what to do about it *when* it surfaces in our hearts. Jesus gives instructions that may surprise you.

Gouging Eyes and Severing Hands

This is where things get interesting. Jesus speaks with a level of extreme urgency, saying the power of lust is so dangerous that it's better to gouge out your eye and cut off your hand than submit to it. Yikes!

There are a few ways people have interpreted this verse. Personally, I don't believe Jesus is recommending literal amputation. He is using hyperbolic language to depict the danger that's presented here. The loss of an eye or a hand is better than losing your whole life.

The reason Jesus talks so directly about adultery and lust is because he knows the damage that comes from it. There is arguably no greater wound than vowing to love someone, only to break that vow through adultery. That is why rebellion in the story of Israel in the Old Testament is often described as marital infidelity. When God's people lusted after idols, they forsook the covenant they promised to keep with God.

As a pastor, I've witnessed how adultery is one of the

most painful issues to walk a couple or family through. I've seen how lust ravages marriages. I've sat in front of individuals screaming in pain after discovering a text message or social media DM detailing an illicit relationship. I've had to console young children and teens reeling from the news of a parent who got caught up in an affair.

Jesus understands the level of pain that comes from lust—in both our human relationships and our relationship with God. We see this in the opening pages of the Bible. In the Garden of Eden, God tells Adam and Eve they can enjoy anything except fruit from one tree.

Soon after, the serpent comes and Adam and Eve begin to see the fruit of the tree lustfully: It was "pleasing to the eye" (Genesis 3:6). They see the tree as a means to an end—to become like God. The moment they take the fruit, sin enters the world. And with sin comes shame, guilt, and fear.

Jesus does not aim to steal our joy and quench our fun. He's helping us guard our joy and live into the goodness of faithful love. How do we do this? Well, this might mean that clear boundaries need to be established—like avoiding certain movies, books, and even places. It means acknowledging our weaknesses and inviting others to help support us on the journey.

It's also important to explore the deeper driving forces beneath it. When you recognize you're using someone else for your own pleasure, there's a deep unmet need driving that compulsion. In this regard, our lust reveals our need for attachment, affection, and communion—with God and others. To help those who struggle to commune with God in everyday life, I wrote *The Deeply Formed Life*, which unpacks five practices that will help you on your journey. As you put these spiritual rhythms into practice—not to become more "spiritual" but to move closer to Jesus—you will come to realize he satisfies you infinitely more than lust can.

Desire and Lust

It's important to clarify that Jesus is not teaching us to be *less sexual*. Many people read this passage and conclude the only way to respond is to deny all sexual longings or view them as dirty. That isn't what Jesus intends. As Christians, we are often embarrassed by our sexual desires and forget that God gives them to us. Sexuality is not the opposite of holiness. Sex, pursued rightly, is not lust.

You're not succumbing to lust if you find a person attractive or if you desire sexual intimacy. It's not lust if you're sexually aroused without any conscious intention to be so. It's not lust if you experience temptation.

Those things are not lust; they're part of being human. When we deny our humanity, vigilance turns into paranoia, and our acts of repression become self-fulfilling prophecies. For many people who have a shame-based theology of sexuality, the goal is to not think about sexual desire. But, ironically, the more you try not to think about it, the more you think about it.

The sexual ethic Jesus teaches is one constructed not on repression but on reordering. He invites us to see our longings for what they are—normal human desires—but calls us to not be driven by our appetites but by love for God and neighbor. As we surrender our lives to this way, we are given grace.

Again, the love of God doesn't *remove* our desires; it *re-orders* them. Unfortunately, in many cases, the church has not done well helping people make sense of their desires. The church has either been silent on the matter or betrayed our witness by forming communities where sexuality is not lived with integrity. I imagine that many of you might be reading these words with great hurt and anger on the inside. If that's you, I want to point to the One who remains steadfast in love. Although the church often fails, God does not.

The Loyalty of God

To align ourselves with the teachings of Jesus is to see his commands from a positive, redemptive perspective. Much like the Ten Commandments, on the other side of "Do not" is "Pursue this." When God says, "Do not murder," he's also saying, "Treat one another with care and dignity." When God says, "Do not covet," he also means, "Live with gratitude and contentment seeing all of life as a gift." When God says, "Do not commit adultery," he's saying, "Let your relationships be characterized by faithful, covenant love."

The fast, easy way of lust circumvents the slow, deep way of love. To pursue love is to disentangle ourselves from the value system of the world that sees our desires as things to be met on demand. The narrow path of Jesus calls us to discern the deeper realities and longing at work in us and to aim our love toward God and neighbor. We see this at work in God's covenantal relationship with his people throughout Scripture.

God wants us to treat others as people made in his image. Why? Because he never betrays us. He doesn't "use" us, although that language is pervasive in church circles. God, in grace, joins his life to ours in faithfulness. We are not used and discarded when our usefulness has expired. God loves and cherishes us until death—and beyond it. His loyal love is most on display in the poured-out acts of Jesus—most significantly, on the cross. It's there he most vividly demonstrates his vow to love us freely, fully, and faithfully. We are not dispensable objects; we are beloved subjects created for lives of communion.

So take heart, friend. The loyalty of God means that your worst moments don't define you. By his grace, you are offered new possibilities to begin again. You might have failed in this area of your life for years, but his love is offered to you at this very moment. This love has the power to move you out of shame and into healing. It helps you name your sins, not with self-protection or condemnation but in the spirit of true repentance. Maybe you were once on the narrow path but have found yourself back on the broad road. Even now, the loyal love of God can fill you with the courage and willingness to step back onto his narrow way. On that road, you will find satisfaction that permeates the core of who you are.

8

OUR MONEY

One morning, I entered a convenience store in Queens to pick up a few items. As I walked in, a man stood in front of the entrance asking for money—a fairly standard occurrence in my neighborhood. I walked in, half ignoring him, to make my purchase. I knew he would be waiting outside, hoping for some loose change or cash, but I had only a ten-dollar bill. To give ten bucks would be outrageous (at least that's what I thought), so upon exiting the store, I lied and said, "Sorry, brother, I don't have any cash on me."

I walked the distance of a block, and when I dug my hand into one of my pockets to take out my car keys, my ten bucks fell out as well. I immediately reached down for it, and as I did, the wind blew it away from me. I took two quick steps to catch it, but another gust carried it a bit farther in the direction of the man in front of the store. At this point, I started trying to catch the bill under my foot, aggressively extending my legs and pounding the sidewalk. After the third attempt, I had the ten dollars under my shoe. I put the money back in my pocket, tapped my thigh twice, and let out a sigh of relief.

When I got into the car, a thought came to mind: *What if God was trying to blow my ten bucks to the man in front of the store?* I pondered that for five seconds, then drove off.

I think about that moment often, not only because I imagine others gawking at me frantically trying to save my cash but because I found myself pulled downward by a power—a power that has that effect on just about all of us. I was chasing my money down the block, making sure it stayed in my pocket and out of someone else's hands.

I know what it's like to pursue money—to be preoccupied with it. In fact, I know what it's like to be captive to it too. I grew up in a home that did not have much in terms of wealth, so I always dreamed of making it big. When I started college, I majored in marketing with one goal: to make *a lot* of money. When that dream didn't immediately come, I turned my gaze to credit card companies, who gave me the illusory power of swiping my card like a boss. Money—and the things money could buy—became a core motivation of my decisions. And becoming a Christian didn't immediately change this.

When I came to faith in Christ, I started watching Christian television preachers who knew how to multiply money by "sowing a seed" (which was a faith promise that I would receive a substantial return on my donation to that preacher's ministry). Their emphasis on getting rich quick piqued my curiosity since I was someone who grew up poor.

When Rosie and I got married in our midtwenties, my

relationship to money was still problematic. We fell into consumer debt very quickly, and it took several years to find freedom from the stranglehold of poor financial decisions.

In all this, it became apparent that money is not just a tool but a power—a dangerous power that can enslave me. And I know I'm not alone.

Let me ask you, what is your relationship with money like? I know I'm meddling a bit, but just between you and me, how are things going? I imagine some of you might say, "Well, I do tithe and support local charities, so I'm doing just fine." Or maybe because you don't have any debt and use a helpful accounting system, you believe money isn't an issue. Or maybe you hear my question and feel shame because even though you can barely pay your monthly bills, you're haunted by the feeling that you should give more. Wherever you are on the spectrum—with financial plenty or lack, an organized budget or zero budget—Jesus has a word for all of us: *mammon*.

Mammon

Mammon refers to "the treasure a person trusts in."[1] Many are quick to point out that the Bible says (correctly, I might add) that it's the *love of money*—not money, per se—that is the root of all evil. That is absolutely right. But here, Jesus gives us needed perspective: Money is not a passive tool; it's a rival god, drawing us into its temple. A god called mammon. Let's look at how Jesus ends this portion of his teaching and then circle back to the start.

Jesus says, "No one can serve two masters. Either you will hate the one and love the other, or you will be devoted to the one and despise the other. You cannot serve both God and money" (Matthew 6:24). Jesus says that worshipping God is an exclusive act—you must worship him and nothing else. It's an interesting statement because there are plenty of other things we can serve at the same time. Dominican theologian Herbert McCabe observed,

> We all know people whose lives are spent in the service of scholarship, or who are dedicated to political liberation, or who are simply head-over-heels in love . . . [but] what Jesus is saying is that if you are serving money . . . then you cannot be serving God.[2]

For Jesus, to serve God and money simultaneously is an impossibility. As John Wesley wrote, you cannot serve both God and mammon comfortably, consistently, and without being contrary.[3]

For Jesus, money exists in a unique category because it's potent. Money is a sign—or *the* sign—of power. It grants access like few things do. It determines who's in and who's out. People sacrifice the well-being of their family for money. Health is compromised in pursuit of money. Integrity is surrendered because of money. Boundaries are crossed because of money. Power is exchanged because of money. Voices are silenced because of money.

Money has a life of its own, animated by the principalities and powers of the world. So yes, it is true that the love of money is the root of all evil. Nonetheless, mammon has a seductive power we must contend with.

When I think about the potential dangers of money, a few rise to the surface.

Money Can Absorb Our Lives

My first observation is how quickly money takes over our lives. Leo Tolstoy, the great Russian novelist, captured this in his short story *How Much Land Does a Man Need?*[4]

In the story, a peasant farmer wants much more than what he has. One day he receives a too-good-to-be-true offer. For only one thousand rubles (currently about eleven American dollars), he can buy all the land his heart desires. The arrangement is that whatever land he walks around in a day becomes his *if* he's back to his starting point by sundown.

The next day, the man moves quickly to cover as much ground as he can. He is exhausted from the walking, but with every step, his territory grows larger. A few hours later, he realizes he is quite far from his starting point, so he starts to run.

As the day fades into night, the farmer sets his eyes on the starting point. Knowing that all the land he's traversed is about to be his, he strenuously crosses the finish line right before the sun sets. Tragically, a few minutes after arriving at the starting point, he collapses and dies. His servants dig a grave that's six feet long and three feet wide. So, how much land does a man need? Just enough to be buried in. (Please don't read this story to your children at bedtime!)

Here's the principle: If we spend the best of our energy and passion to gain wealth, it ends up owning us. When our lives are absorbed with money and what it can get us, we end up serving it to our own demise. Our lives are to be caught up in loving attentiveness to God. Our decisions are to be guided by the inner witness of the Spirit. Our ethics are to be shaped by the values of the kingdom.

Right before Jesus warns us about Master Money, he has a word about our eyes: "If your eyes are healthy, your whole body will be full of light. But if your eyes are unhealthy, your whole body will be full of darkness. If then the light within you is darkness, how great is that darkness!" (Matthew 6:22–23).

The context here is not illicit sexual material but insatiable money pursuit. Healthy eyes are fixed on the pursuit of God's priorities. Unhealthy eyes are fixed on the priority of the money god. Jesus longs for you to live with clear eyes, not clouded vision.

Money Clouds Moral Judgment

Whether it's Judas betraying Jesus, or large corporations creating the conditions for a recession based on greed, money has a way of clouding judgment. I remember a conversation I had with a fellow pastor. His notoriety skyrocketed because of his ability to speak to polarizing issues with moral clarity, shaped by Scripture. His prophetic voice was not accepted by all, but he was increasingly being invited to large, wealthy spaces to speak on a myriad of issues. He landed a book deal and purchased a home. He later shared his fear that he wouldn't be able to pay his mortgage if he offended the wrong people.

My friend Steve shared a similar story from a trusted mentor. After Steve purchased a home, his mentor warned him that purchasing a home very easily leads to watering down one's prophetic gift. Why? Because speaking truth to power sometimes means that the comfort that money secures is jeopardized. That is something I ponder weekly.

When I was financially struggling, I had no reservations about speaking truth. When I became financially comfortable, I noticed a newfound hesitation to proclaim hard things.

When money becomes the goal of our lives, we start saying things (or withhold saying things) instead of obeying Jesus. When that happens, our moral convictions become influenced by a power outside God's kingdom.

Money Damages Relationships

Few things divide people like money. Marriages are often damaged because of a couple's inability to navigate all the underlying stressors and values that money reveals. When transactions around money occur within friendships, a subtle dynamic is introduced that has the power to change it forever. And of course, money has a way of altering our perspective of people, leading us to treat some with favor while ignoring others.

In the first century, money created a culture of hierarchical elitism that damaged the witness of the early church. The apostle James wrote these important words that are still needed two thousand years later:

My brothers and sisters, believers in our glorious Lord Jesus Christ must not show favoritism. Suppose a man comes into your meeting wearing a gold ring and fine clothes, and a poor man in filthy old clothes also comes in. If you show special attention to the man wearing fine clothes and say, "Here's a good seat for you," but say to the poor man, "You stand there" or "Sit on the floor by my feet," have you not discriminated among yourselves and become judges with evil thoughts? (James 2:1–4)

Jesus came to establish a human community that resists assigning value to people based on wealth. In Christ, the dividing wall that regarded some as worthy and others as unworthy was effectively destroyed in his death and resurrection. The money god is still thriving today, promising status and favor, but God has given us many defenses. One that may surprise you is baptism, which may seem disconnected from the topic of wealth. Since the conception of the church, baptism has been a countercultural act that unites believers and pushes back the influence of mammon.

When I was baptized as a twenty-year-old, my church didn't give me a T-shirt with their logo on it. Instead, I received a long white garment. It was like I was graduating from high school again. The baptismal garment signified that I was made pure and new in Jesus. To that I say, "Amen!"

Everyone baptized in my church received the same white garment, which signifies that baptism isn't simply an act of individual piety; it's a creator of communal identity. Whatever you happen to wear on the day of your baptism (whether an expensive suit or tattered clothes), you exchange it for a garment that everyone looks the same in. This does not eliminate your uniqueness but celebrates your equal standing before God. It's a physical reinforcement of a spiritual reality: We are all one in Christ.

To serve God is to do away with superficial hierarchies that bestow value on some people but not others. To serve mammon is to assign value and dignity based on bank accounts, houses, cars, and accomplishments. Thank good-ness Jesus ushers us into something far more beautiful.

The question is, what does it look like for us to kneel before Jesus in this area of our lives? I suggest three things: generosity, simplicity, and Sabbath economics.

Generosity

One of the primary ways we denounce mammon is by shar-ing it with others. This doesn't mean we can't save or in-vest, but every time we part with our money to serve another, we take another step on the path of Jesus. Put an-other way, generosity refuses to step off the path onto the self-serving wasteland of the broad path.

Here's an important truth in Jesus's kingdom: Generos-ity is not a return-on-investment strategy. We do not give to double our income; we give because God has been gra-cious to us and calls us to serve our neighbor. Contrary to many prosperity teachers who peddle generosity as a get-rich-quick initiative, being generous doesn't control God's hand; it's the act of opening ours.

Throughout my life, there have been times when I was generous with my money and noticed financial provision thereafter. There have also been times I didn't give gener-ously and God still blessed me. Generosity doesn't manipu-late God's grace; it's about living free from attachments. As Jesus says in the Sermon on the Mount, God "causes his sun to rise on the evil and the good, and sends rain on the righteous and the unrighteous" (Matthew 5:45). In other words, our goodness doesn't compel God to be good. He is good because he is good.

Every Sunday at New Life Fellowship, we recite a prayer of generosity. It reminds us every week of God's provision, the deceptive nature of mammon, and our duty to steward our possessions for the kingdom. Here it is:

> Father, you are an abundant giver.
> There is nothing that we have that you have
> not given us.
> The way of your kingdom is the way of
> generosity.
> Help us to honor you with our resources.
> Free us from the deceit of riches.
> Lead us on the path of generosity.
> For your glory, Lord, for the abundance
> of our own lives and for the sake of
> others. AMEN.[5]

Every time I mindfully recite that prayer, I'm given a new perspective on money. I need this perspective because, honestly, I secretly fear not having enough. Can you relate? Jesus understands this and, thankfully, right after this section on treasure, he teaches about worry and anxiety. (More on this in the next chapter.)

Few things produce more anxiety than money. It's easy to believe that greed and hoarding money are rooted in selfishness. Many times, they're actually symptoms of fear. Some of us cling to money because we are afraid of having nothing. Maybe you grew up in a home that struggled financially. You experienced pain and difficulty. Now you live with an internalized script of scarcity, believing that resources are always on the verge of running out. Something in your heart warns you that letting go of your assets is a recipe for poverty. As a pastor, I've had candid conversations with people who were very successful but because of the struggle of their immigrant parents, they live in great fear that one day they, too, could lose everything.

Generosity, which looks different from person to person, is part of the narrow path. Jesus wants you to see that your well-being is secured not by acquiring but by relinquishing. Trust him in that.

Simplicity

When Rosie and I decided to turn our attention to freeing ourselves from credit card debt, it started with simplicity. We knew we had to live within our means, which meant cutting out the fast-and-loose approach we had toward spending. It also meant we had to get rid of some things—especially expensive furniture—that put us in this position in the first place.

When we got married, we both had Pottery Barn taste even though we had thrift-shop money. That hurdle didn't stop us from swiping cards with smiles on our faces. In particular, I remember a beautiful dark-brown wooden desk. Sure, it cost more than our monthly rent, but it looked so nice, so we bought it (and a coffee table and shelves to boot!). I lemon-Pledged the surface of that desk every couple of days. It always had a shine to it.

Later, as we were being crushed under the weight of debt, we knew we had to simplify our lives, so we started selling furniture we didn't need. My beloved desk was the first item we decided to unload. I'll never forget the day.

We went on Craigslist and posted a picture of it. I was

sure no one would buy it for the price we were offering, but, alas, within thirty minutes, a woman responded, saying she would be at our apartment within two hours. I started to grieve.

She arrived with a personal assistant and paid us the money, but her assistant needed help getting *my* cherished Pottery Barn desk into her van. Not only was I losing something I loved, but I also had to pick up that heavy item and lug it down a few flights of stairs. Simplicity is certainly not easy.

Simplicity is not just about limiting clutter in our homes; it's primarily about reducing the disorder of our hearts. It's a commitment to prioritizing the way of Jesus. This is why he uses the words *treasures* and *heart* in this section. He says,

> Do not store up for yourselves treasures on earth, where moths and vermin destroy, and where thieves break in and steal. But store up for yourselves treasures in heaven, where moths and vermin do not destroy, and where thieves do not break in and steal. For where your treasure is, there your heart will be also. (Matthew 6:19–21)

To store up treasures in heaven doesn't mean that upon death, we will have special access to a celestial storage facility brimming with precious jewels, like some sort of Jack Sparrow loot lair. Rather, it's a way of saying pleasing God and not hoarding stuff must be what drives us. Dale Bruner said, "Jesus counsels us to make it our ambition to be a success before the Father, . . . to accumulate the rewards and treasures of *his* notice and esteem."[6]

Simplicity is difficult but purifying. We let go of the clutter of our hearts to gain the freedom of God. In his classic book *Celebration of Discipline*, Richard Foster noted ten aspects of simplicity that deserve mention:

1. Buy things for their usefulness rather than their status.

2. Reject anything that is producing an addiction in you.

3. Develop a habit of giving things away.

4. Refuse to be propagandized by the custodians of gadgetry.

5. Learn to enjoy things without owning them.

6. Develop a deeper appreciation for the creation.

7. Look with a healthy skepticism at all "buy now, pay later" schemes.

8. Obey Jesus's instructions about plain, honest speech.

9. Reject anything that breeds the oppression of others.

10. Shun anything that distracts you from seeking first the kingdom of God.[7]

I carry this list in one of my Bibles as a reminder to keep my heart free from the insidious pull of money and possessions. Some of the instructions are harder than others for me (I really enjoy good gadgetry), but I'm constantly on a journey toward stewarding the resources God entrusts to me.

Sabbath Economics

I'll mention one final way to push back the power of mammon: practicing Sabbath. The habit of pausing from work—aka, making money—is a subversive revolt against the money god. Sabbath creates conditions where all can rest from the tyranny of work.

I have been guilty of seeing Sabbath keeping as an individual or family practice that focuses exclusively on our well-being. And yes, that's a major part of it. However, Sabbath is about resistance just as much as it's about rest—resisting a culture that works people to death, taking advantage of their labor.

As followers of Jesus, we are not just called to eliminate debt, budget well, and give generously. We are also invited to create conditions where those around us can rest from a culture of materialism, consumerism, and unbridled capitalism. Old Testament scholar Walter Brueggemann wrote,

> The way of *mammon* (capital, wealth) is the way of commodity, which is the way of endless desire, endless productivity, and endless restlessness without any Sabbath. . . . The "choice of gods" is, in context, a choice of restlessness or restfulness.[8]

When we keep Sabbath, we choose to orient our lives around the God who gives rest, not the god (mammon) who keeps us restless. This is for not just our own lives but those under our care and leadership too.

Don't miss this: Sabbath is a move toward social compassion and justice. In the Old Testament, when God commands his people to rest, the entire community (including servants and animals) is included. This is his way of protecting his people from the spirit of Pharaoh, who mercilessly worked them to the bone. Ironically, without Sabbath, his people are tempted to re-create that oppressive environment. We face the same temptation today.

Practically, this means finding savvy ways to form just and equitable environments. It means paying people fairly. It means resisting economic exploitation in our communities (for example, the rampant gentrification in urban contexts that displaces longtime residents). It also means making spaces for people to be free from the burden of poverty. As one of our pastors, Redd Sevilla, has said, the Bible is clear that Jesus loves the poor but doesn't love poverty. Sabbath reminds us that God created rest for all. And if we can't rest, it means that we are still under Pharaoh's grip.

Jesus challenges us to step into larger conversations around the way the money god helps or harms people. Our congregation has partnered with several other churches in Queens to push back against gentrification that displaces lifelong neighbors. We've established programs to provide seed capital to people who have big dreams but little cash. To faithfully follow Jesus in this area means we must tackle financial practices on individual, interpersonal, and institutional levels. Where are the less fortunate people around you? How is God calling you to help them? How can you resist mammon's oppression and bring the restful relief of Jesus—not merely in prayer (as important as that is), but with your time, treasures, and talent?

Dethroning Mammon

Dethroning mammon is an uphill battle. Talking openly about money is taboo. Author Richard Foster noted, "In a survey of psychotherapists in which they listed things they should not do with their patients, it was found that lending a client money was a greater taboo than touching, kissing, or even sexual intercourse."[9]

That's the kind of power money has. And yet, there's a greater power available to you.

The gospel of Jesus offers a life that doesn't heed mammon's mandates. The gospel has the power to free you for God and the way of his kingdom—a kingdom that redefines what liberation and value truly entail. On the broad path, the money god subjects you to perpetual restlessness in the name of "progress" and "fulfillment." On the narrow path, you can live at ease in God's loving care. Isn't that what you yearn for? Aren't you longing for ease over restlessness? Jesus offers this to you.

On the narrow road, money starts to lose its grip on your life. That might feel like a crushing loss at first as you relinquish control of your assets and surrender them for kingdom purposes. But over time, you will celebrate the freedom it brings—to you and others. To use money for good, rather than letting it use you, is a thrilling way to live.

As you think about loosening your grip on money, worry and anxiety are likely bubbling up inside you. Thankfully, that is exactly what Jesus talks about next, so let's follow him there.

OUR ANXIETY

As a parent, worrying is a full-time job. When I first became a father, it went something like this:

We find out we're expecting a baby. (Me: *Woo-hoo!*)

We start going to scheduled doctor's appointments. *(Is everything okay?)*

We get closer to the due date. *(What if my wife's water breaks and we're stuck in traffic? I might have to deliver the baby.)*

The baby is born. *(What do we do now?)*

The baby is sleeping. *(Is the baby still breathing?)*

The toddler starts crawling. *(We better childproof every light socket.)*

The toddler is not as articulate as the other kids on the playground. *(Oh no, my child has developmental challenges.)*

The babysitter comes over. *(Let's just cancel date night.)*

And that's only the first eighteen months!

Many years later, I wish I could tell you I've overcome worry. Truth be told, I'm a recovering worrier. One time my young son asked me, "Do you mean *warrior,* Dad?" Nope, worrier. To say I'm recovering is to celebrate the progress I've made in this area, but in a given moment, worry can manifest in a New York second. (For those unfamiliar with the term, it's the period of time between a traffic light turning green and the cab behind you honking.)

Worry, or anxiety (I'll use them interchangeably), makes the world go round. It's the impetus behind much of our commerce and decision making. It pays the bills of news outlets and corporations. In the words of the late journalist Eric Sevareid, "The biggest big business in America is not steel, automobiles or television. It is the manufacture, refinement and distribution of anxiety."[1]

The struggle with worry is universal. We worry about our bills, our health, our children, our work, our relationships, our safety, our futures, our [fill in the blank]. Concerns around anxiety continue to skyrocket. In a 2022 report, the American Psychological Association detailed this alarming news:

> Around seven in 10 adults (72%) have experienced additional health impacts due to stress, including feeling overwhelmed (33%), experiencing changes in sleeping habits (32%), and/or worrying constantly (30%).[2]

Almost one out of every three adults is habitually anxious. The good news is, Jesus offers help. There's a section break between the previous topic of money (mammon) and worry, but Jesus intends to show how they're connected. A life oriented around mammon always leads to worry. Worry is not reserved for those barely making ends meet; it's also a struggle for those who have more than enough. In fact, the greater worrier might be the one who has more to lose than the one who is looking for a little to get by.

Into this atmosphere of anxiety, Jesus says, "Do not worry about your life, what you will eat or drink; or about your body, what you will wear" (Matthew 6:25).

When Jesus tells his followers not to worry, he interrupts the continuous loop of what-ifs that tend to dominate our lives. To *feel* worry and anxiety are normal parts of being human; however, to *feed* worry and anxiety leads to bondage. We were not made to be imprisoned in this way. And yet, it can be so difficult to find the off-ramp.

In the fall of 2013, I woke up with pain on one side of my neck and swollen glands underneath my jawline. I figured I had some kind of infection. Within a few days, I had swollen lymph nodes all over my body, a few of them a bit smaller than ping-pong balls. On top of that, I started having night sweats, lost my appetite, and felt sluggish. I went to my doctor to have tests run. There was nothing conclusive. That's when my worry *really* kicked in.

For multiple days, I silently ruminated on all that *could* go wrong. I lost countless hours of sleep and had little strength to open my Bible. After a few weeks, I was diagnosed with lymphatic tuberculosis. When I look back at that season, I realize how easy it was to feed the worry monster within. I had legitimate concerns, but I wouldn't let anyone in and found myself resisting the spiritual, emotional, and relational resources at my disposal.

Ruminating on potential trouble chokes the life out of many people. Jesus knows this. He knows your world—with all your responsibilities, worries, fears, and hopes—and wants to let some oxygen in the room. Ready to breathe again? Let's listen to Jesus together.

Birds and Flowers

Jesus highlights three areas of human life: eating, drinking, and clothing. While it's worthwhile to examine these aspects of existence, I believe that Jesus is using them as shorthand for the regular stuff of life. He's highlighting the daily realities that concern us most, the things we need to make life work. Surprisingly, Jesus says that these things are *not* what life is all about. He says, "Is not life more than food, and the body more than clothes?" (Matthew 6:25). When I first read these words, I heard a dismissive tone in Jesus—one that minimizes the plight of the poor. For people who wonder where their next meal will come from, it can sound callous when someone with a full belly downplays worry. I don't aim to dismiss the pain of those struggling to meet their basic needs.

But this is Jesus we're talking about. Looking at the entirety of his life and teaching, it's obvious he *would never* dismiss the plight of the poor. Instead he clarifies that a life oriented around possessions is a life of anxiety. Much like his words in the Our Father (the Lord's Prayer) about daily bread, Jesus calls his followers to a carefree and content life. He is not saying that food, drink, and clothing are unimportant; he's saying they can't be *ultimate*.

A Carefree Existence

To make his point (as the master teacher he is), Jesus points his listeners to the sky. He calls his followers to a carefree existence that mirrors the daily habits of birds. Instead of worry and anxiety, carefree spirituality should be what characterizes people who live under the rule and reign of Jesus.

Many of us hear the word *carefree* in negative ways. It sounds reckless and irresponsible. It gives the image of someone with their head in the clouds. Or it communicates the naïve childlikeness of those avoiding the drudgery of so-called adulting. But what if the unworried way of children is actually the *key* to following Jesus? What if it's possible to live responsibly while also rejecting worry? How do we even arrive at this point?

As I write this, there's a leak in one of the pipes in our basement, causing problems with our boiler. It's wintertime. It's getting cold. This might cost us some serious money to fix. Even now, I'm holding on to this teaching from Jesus. We need to research and find a solution, but Rosie and I are asking for the grace to entrust this to the Father. Note what I'm not doing or suggesting: I'm not ignoring the problem, believing it will fix itself, nor am I avoiding the frustration and concern this brings to our home. I'm releasing my worry to God, trusting him to provide.

Jesus calls us to imitate the birds. Have you observed them? They fly here and there. They perch on top of homes and search for their own daily bread. They do not anxiously fret about tomorrow. I know what you're thinking: Birds have tiny brains. They lack the capacity to fret and worry.

Then again, maybe that is Jesus's point. To live under God's provision strips worry of its power. Perhaps we know *too much*. Just maybe the sparrows are onto something.

Jesus takes it even further in his next illustration. He calls us to examine the flowers of the field. The birds actively search for sustenance, without freaking out, but the flowers just stand there. They don't stay up all night wondering if they will be clothed in botanical splendor; they just exist. God adorns fields with their beauty and abundance as a reminder that, as he clothes them, he will clothe us. We can let go of our cares. We can stop our striving. Jesus places reminders of his provision all around us—in the air and in the field—so the question is, are we paying attention?

Contentment

There is much on the broad path to distract us from God's faithfulness. Jesus describes this path, saying that Gentiles (in this context, those not living under the gracious rule of God's kingdom) ceaselessly chase material things (see Matthew 6:32). They are possessed by possessions. Obsessed with objects. Anxious over attainments. Life is dominated by running after these things. For Jesus, this is a tragic existence.

The worry that fills many of our hearts focuses not just on what we don't have in seasons of scarcity but also on what we don't have in moments of provision. It's easy to assume (when times are good) that contentment will come. Not the case. For example, I remember how much I loved my third car. My first car, a 1989 Oldsmobile Royale, was purchased from my uncle. (By the way, I didn't get the nephew discount.) It was like driving a tank. After three months, it died on me. My second car was a tiny 1988 Nissan Sentra, purchased from a brother at church. (I didn't get the brother-in-Christ discount, either.) It was like driving a Matchbox car. After four months, it passed away too. I saved some money and purchased a 1995 Nissan Altima. I loved it. I took multiple pictures with it. Shined the tires. Winked at myself in the rearview mirror. I rejoiced over God's provision. All was good and well until I ran into a friend who was driving . . . a Jaguar. Suddenly my coveting heart longed for status and success. I needed a Jaguar too! (This example has played out in a myriad of other ways in my life.)

To perpetually strive after more introduces anxiety into our systems. The alternative, found only on the narrow path, is contentment. Contentment involves living free from the lie that having more makes you something more. Whether the more is money, homes, titles, social media followers, or power, Jesus invites us to detached lives, where the stuff we own doesn't own us. That doesn't necessarily mean we must forfeit all property, but it *does* mean we must develop a relaxed indifference toward possessions—one that isn't elated or depressed when they come and go.

How can we live that way? Jesus doesn't offer a formula to follow—no ten steps to success here. Instead, he shows us a new way to see God.

False Images of God

The images we have of God in our heads determine the degree of worry we feel in our souls. No tool or set of steps—no matter how catchy or innovative—can pry us away from worry if we don't live in this truth: God is with us and for us. Please read that again. It is one of the most important aspects of Jesus's life and teachings. Jesus wants us to think of God as *Abba,* the compassionate and fully present One who cares for his children.

On many Saturday mornings, I make pancakes: delicious pancakes from scratch, as God intended. My family loves them! My children eat more than I can count. It's almost like they believe there's an endless supply. Their trust—that Dad will provide more than enough—reminds me of these words from Richard Foster, who describes making pancakes for *his* children:

> Not once did I see them slipping some into a pocket, thinking, "I don't know about Dad; I'd better put away a little stash so that I can be sure of pancakes tomorrow." As far as they were concerned, the reservoir of pancakes was infinite. . . . All they needed to do was ask and . . . they would receive. They lived in trust.[3]

When Jesus arrives at this part of his kingdom manifesto, he wants us to know something about God: He is trustworthy. This is a truth we need to hear again and again. Our Father has an endless supply of love and compassion for us. As someone who grew up without much financially, I can easily slip into a state of worry, believing that God's resources will run out on me. But hear Jesus's encouragement: God has an endless supply of goodness aimed your way.

Let's unpack some of the breathtaking truths about

God's provision. First, Scripture teaches that *God's generosity extends to everyone*: "He causes his sun to rise on the evil *and* the good" (Matthew 5:45). God is a merciful, forgiving parent who pours out love on prodigal and self-righteous sons alike. Jesus committed his life to showcasing what God is like. When we look upon him, we behold the Father. He wants to make sure the world knows the care and concern that permeates the heart of God.

Second, though God is infinite in knowledge and power, he cares for the minute details of his creation. Instead of coldly observing the cosmos, the Creator lovingly tends to it. Even little birds, insignificant in the scope of the universe, are fed by their heavenly Father (see 6:26). The unseen God extends his cosmic hands to provide for pigeons. The same is true of the grass and flowers: Every blade and petal is handcrafted and sustained by the Provider. Like he does for the birds and flora, God actively holds our lives together. In fact, he's *much more* involved with us.

Is there a false image of God you've embraced—one that denies he can provide? Be reminded, he *delights* in providing! Through Jesus's words in the Sermon on the Mount, the Holy Spirit can heal the false images of God warping our reality. I love how author Brennan Manning put it:

The Spirit of God is the great unmasker of illusions, the great destroyer of icons and idols. God's love for us is so great that He does not permit us to harbor false images, no matter how attached we are to them. God strips those falsehoods from us no matter how naked it may make us, because it is better to live naked in truth than clothed in fantasy.[4]

I know what it's like to have images of God in my mind that don't align with what Jesus taught and embodied. I had a youth pastor who had an uncanny ability (if that's what you want to call it) to discern *why* a person fell upon hard times. His formula was quite simple: If something bad happened to someone, he claimed that the judgment of God was visiting them. If a brother from the church fell ill, this "prophetic" person would explain, "That's what happens when you stop going to church." I became paranoid that if I sinned, God would turn on me and crush me under his celestial thumb.

The images we carry live deep in our subconscious. In fact, I've discovered them in surprising ways. When my two-year-old son was hospitalized with febrile seizures, one of my first thoughts was, *My son is sick because I haven't prayed enough.* I know that is not true. Still, that image of a punitive God was stored away and surfaced under deep stress. When I contracted a strange case of tuberculosis in my lymph nodes, I wondered if it was some kind of divine punishment.

I don't ruminate on these images and scripts consciously, but they live in me. Deeply. Through practices of spiritual formation and discipleship, these lies can be rooted out of our theology. Maybe you carry worry and anxiety about God's posture toward you. I did for years. Slowly but surely, I've realized that Jesus doesn't cause worry; he removes it. He longs to do the same for you.

Jesus wants you to know him as tender, not terrorizing; cruciform in love, not capricious; compassionate, not condemning; attentive, not aloof. Maybe you've lived for a long while with an image of God in your head that causes anxiety. Please, behold Jesus and his tenderness. Today you can begin a new journey of seeing God. His love for you is steadfast and unrelenting.

The sad truth is, worry steals time. Jesus says, "Can any one of you by worrying add a single hour to your life?" (Matthew 6:27). Translation: Stop worrying and start enjoying. The more you worry, the less time you have. Helpfully, Jesus doesn't merely say to stop worrying; he tells us to seek his kingdom.

Seek First the Kingdom

Jesus says, "Seek first his kingdom and his righteousness, and all these things will be given to you as well" (Matthew 6:33). What does it mean to seek the kingdom? And how does this pursuit lead to a worry-free existence?

I've heard many people interpret this exhortation like this: *Put God first and everything else will fall into place.* Sounds nice, but in practice it usually means praying more, going to church, and reading the Bible (things I encourage people to do every week). I often cringe when I hear people say they are "putting God first," because it often means doing external, spiritual stuff without overhauling the larger system that forms our lives. I've learned that it is possible to "keep God first" and be racist; to "keep God first" and succumb to greed; to "keep God first" and adopt worldly understandings of success. Clearly, that is not what Jesus means.

As I've spent time with the entirety of Jesus's teaching in the Sermon on the Mount, I've begun to pick up on what I think he's getting at. To seek God's kingdom first is to have our entire value system transformed, or at least questioned.

It is to view God in a new light—one marked by compassionate care.

It means we view our possessions through a new lens, seeing them as gifts to be shared and stewarded for the blessing of others rather than as things to be stockpiled.

It means we look at our lives with a fresh perspective, seeing ourselves as beloved children, not faceless and nameless objects.

One way to seek the kingdom of God is to identify how we seek other kingdoms and strategies in pursuit of the good life. For example, when Rosie and I sit down for our monthly home-finance meeting (the most challenging meeting of the month because of everything money represents), we begin our time in prayer, asking the Holy Spirit to help us be on guard against all the ways we have been deformed by our families and culture. When we look at all the needs before us, the bills to pay, and the hopes we have, if we're not careful, we slip into bad habits. We start spending flippantly. We fearfully withhold generosity. However, when we step back, pray, and communicate with each other, God's presence guides and reassures us.

As we situate ourselves in God's world and ways, worry no longer has a grip on our souls, and we begin to discern the gifts of God already at our disposal. With open hands, we find ourselves caught and carried by the strong and loving arms of the Father. This is an image the words of beloved author Henri Nouwen have helped me grasp.

One day, Nouwen went to the circus and spent time with the acrobats to see what he could learn about spirituality. He engaged in conversation with a flying trapeze artist. Nouwen was curious as to how they were so successful in performing their dangerous feats. Here's how their conversation went:

> "As a flyer, I must have complete trust in my catcher. The public might think that I am the great star of the trapeze, but the real star is Joe, my catcher. He has to be there for me with split-second precision and grab me out of the air as I come to him in the long jump." "How does it work?" Nouwen asked. "The secret," he said, "is that the flyer does nothing and the catcher does everything. When I fly to Joe, I have simply to stretch out my arms and hands and wait for him to catch me and pull me safely over the apron behind the catchbar." "You do nothing!" Nouwen said, surprised. "Nothing," Rodleigh repeated. . . . "A flyer must fly, and a catcher must catch, and the flyer must trust, with outstretched arms, that his catcher will be there for him."[5]

Jesus is letting us know that the Father is our catcher. Our lives are safe in his providing hands. But first we must let go of worldly values that stand opposed to God's kingdom.

To let go of the value system of the world is unnerving. Orienting our lives around Jesus and his kingdom can feel impractical. But isn't much of our worry a result of grasping the world's definition of happiness and success? So, let me ask you the following questions:

- Who or what is shaping your definition of significance?

- What specific actions, decisions, postures, and habits will help you seek God's kingdom in this season? Be as specific as possible.

- How are you seeking the kingdom of the world over the kingdom of God?

Jesus invites you onto the narrow path, where you can live at ease, confident in God's provision. In addition to your physical needs, deeper soul provision is available as well. God's grace can form you to live as his child, joyfully content with the gifts he's given. His Spirit can shape you to live openhandedly—not grasping or comparing, but living in gratitude under God's care. Like he does for the birds scattered in the sky, God invites you into the carefree spaciousness of life with him. There is no better place to be.

10

OUR JUDGMENTS

Human beings are judging machines. Isn't that why we love shows like *American Idol*? Or maybe I should speak for myself. I've spent hours watching these kinds of talent shows because it gives me an opportunity, in the privacy of my own home, to scrutinize others. To sit in the judge's seat. To text in my vote (which I did once) and declare who is worthy of advancing.

But that is not the only place judgment surfaces. It's a common, repeated occurrence in our day-to-day lives. As a New Yorker, I pride myself in parallel parking. When I see someone really struggling to angle their car into a space, I sigh and shake my head.

When we judge, we position ourselves in a favorable light, looking for any edge we can find to prop ourselves up.

Or we judge because it makes us feel powerful, even if no one else recognizes our dominance. Our quickness to judge reveals a gap in our apprenticeship to Jesus.

 In his book *Repenting of Religion,* Gregory Boyd told of a time when he was at the mall on a Saturday afternoon, sipping a Coke and observing people. He noted his penchant for casually judging others:

> I notice that some are pretty and some are not. Some are slender; some are obese. On the basis of what they wear, their facial expressions, the way they relate to their spouses, friends, or kids, I conclude some are "godly" while others are "ungodly." Some give me a warm feeling as I watch their tenderness toward their children. Others make me angry or disgusted.
>
> Then suddenly I notice *I'm noticing all of this.* After a moment's introspection I realize [that my judging of others] is making me feel good. . . . It's satisfying some need I have to stand in judgment over people. . . . I enjoy being the one who . . . gets to pronounce the verdict: Pretty. Ugly. Good figure. Fat. Godly. Ungodly. Disgusting. Cute. And so on.
>
> With this insight came another, this one, I am sure, prompted by the Holy Spirit. I recalled that Jesus taught wherever we go, our first responsibility is to bless people. . . .
>
> So I stopped. I determined to have one thought, and one thought only, about every person I saw in the mall on that afternoon: it was to love them and bless them as people uniquely created by God who have infinite worth because Jesus died for them.[1]

I don't know about you, but I have had a similar experience. I have been quick to judge—speedy in my criticism, condemning others inwardly in an instant.

When someone pushes back on something I post on social media, my initial response is one of judgment rather than curiosity. When I drive in my neighborhood during a local or national election season and see a sign on someone's lawn supporting a particular candidate, my head shakes and my eyes roll. When I see parents unable to calm or control their kids, I make unfair assumptions about their parenting.

It's remarkable how quickly we categorize people without knowing their stories—often without knowing their names or anything else, for that matter. It's tragic how an assumption grows into full-fledged pronouncement without really knowing another person's heart.

Smartphones and social media have fueled this impulse. For all the good our devices can do, they have discipled many of us into dehumanizing judgmentalism.

Don't like a line in someone's bio? Judgment.

Someone liked an article you found distasteful? Judgment.

Someone is following a person you find abhorrent? Double judgment.

The temptation to judge is literally found in our pockets.

Judging others is pervasive because it helps us classify people into categories that help us make sense of the world the way we see it. Religious folks, especially, tend to carry a black-or-white dualism that makes it easy to determine who is in and who is out of God's favor. But humanity is far more complex than that. We are all a mixed bag. We don't see others with the clarity we think we do. Whether we're participating in racial profiling, theorizing about another person's salvation, or assuming why someone didn't respond to our email, Jesus wants to teach us how to withhold judgment.

In 2015, Barna reported that

> a significant number of young adults have deeper complaints about church. More than one-third say their negative perceptions are a result of moral failures in church leadership (35%). And substantial majorities of Millennials who don't go to church say they see Christians as judgmental (87%), hypocritical (85%), anti-homosexual (91%) and insensitive to others (70%).[2]

How tragic, when the very thing Jesus tells his followers to avoid is the thing they're notorious for!

As a pastor, I occasionally have conversations with congregants who want me to be *more* judgmental. In one email, someone wrote, "Pastor, we need to hear more sermons from you on God's judgment."

I replied, "Almost every week, I preach about the Judge who was judged in our place."

The congregant responded, "I know you do, but not *that* kind of judgment."

What was going on here? Very simply, this person wanted me to classify right and wrong in a way that stoked fear. That is the evangelistic impulse for judgment. But if we think the gospel of Jesus can be faithfully proclaimed only through the language of fear, judgment, and intimidation, we have profoundly misunderstood it. Certainly, there is a place for warning. In fact, the prophets of the Old Testament, John the Baptist, Paul, and Jesus offer many warnings to people who have lived in unloving, self-oriented ways. The problem is, it's easy to imagine we're joining the ranks of biblical prophets when we pronounce judgment, when much of the time, it's just self-righteous.

In the Gospels, Jesus deals with this condemning impulse in his own disciples. Once, as Jesus journeys to Jerusalem, the people of a Samaritan village refuse to offer hospitality to him and his disciples (which was a huge slight in ancient culture). In response, James and John nonchalantly ask, "Lord, do you want us to call fire down from heaven to destroy them?" (Luke 9:54). Immediately Jesus turns and rebukes them. This is a word for Christians in every age. We are to be known not for our judgment but for our grace; not for our faultfinding but our love; not for our smug criticism but our loving discernment. Jesus commands us to do so.

How do we avoid being judgmental? There are two kinds of judgmentalism I want to unpack: existential and eschatological. These are just fancy ways of saying we can't judge a person's heart or eternal destination. Let's look at each briefly.

Existential Judgment
(Judging Another Person's Heart)

We are not God. We don't know the inner workings of another person's heart. I think about what God says to Samuel while looking for a king to lead Israel: "The LORD does not look at the things people look at. People look at the outward appearance, but the LORD looks at the heart" (1 Samuel 16:7).

We find ourselves in a lot of trouble when we presume

to know the motivations of another person. Withholding judgment is not merely a moral act; it's a theological one because it means humbly accepting we are not God. The primary calling for followers of Jesus is to show up in love, truth, and grace, not draw conclusions about the interior condition of other people.

Eschatological Judgment (Judging Another Person's Final Destination)

When Jesus tells us not to judge, he doesn't mean we are to withhold all judgment (a human impossibility); he instructs us not to pass *final* judgment on a person. Again, that's God's prerogative, not ours.

The tendency for many of us is to make claims—out loud or in our heads—about who is saved and who is not. When Jesus tells us not to judge, he's letting us know that we are in no position to determine what the final spiritual condition of a person will be. God alone is the righteous judge who will adjudicate.

During a forum at Harvard's Kennedy School of Government, someone asked Billy Graham a question:

> "Dr. Graham, Jesus said, 'I am the way, the truth and the life and no man cometh unto the Father but by me.' Doesn't that mean that all non-Christians, including the Jews, are going to hell?"
>
> Graham replied, "God will judge us all. This is a God of love and mercy, but also of justice. We will all come before the judgment of God, and I am so glad that God has that job and I don't."

The young questioner looked disappointed. "Could you tell us what you think God is going to say?"

Graham answered, "Well, God doesn't consult with me on things like that." The despondent questioner walked away.[3]

We are in dangerous territory when we dare to judge another person's heart or forecast the final destiny of another, yet there *is* a type of judgment Jesus condones.

Judging with Integrity

Before we get to what God-approved judgment looks like, Jesus gives a warning: "In the same way you judge others, you will be judged, and with the measure you use, it will be measured to you" (Matthew 7:2). In other words, what goes around comes around.

Jesus knows that on a purely human level, whenever someone dishes out condemnation or harsh judgment on another, chances are that judgment will come back with great force. For example, someone who constantly criticizes others is bound to *be* criticized. On a deeper (and eternal) level, God's standard for judging us is based on how we treat others. Ask yourself, *How harshly do I judge others in my heart and mind?* This should temper our judgmentalism because at some point, in this life or the next, our day is coming.

Beyond the warning, Jesus names why our judgments often go awry: We judge others without clear eyes. Even worse, we judge others with massive pieces of lumber sticking out of our eyes.

He says, "Why do you look at the speck of sawdust in

your brother's eye and pay no attention to the plank in your own eye?" (verse 3). Pay close attention to the principle: Judgment that doesn't start with yourself is hypocrisy. A term to summarize this principle is *self-examination*. If you truly desire to avoid the trap of hypocrisy and harsh judgmentalism, this concept will help you immensely.

Howard Thurman, a civil rights leader and spiritual mentor to Martin Luther King, Jr., shared an anecdote that captured this concept well. One day while he was at a university for a summer speaking event, one of the attendees complained that he couldn't sleep because his roommate snored terribly. The man came to Thurman's door irritated by his roommate's obnoxious volume. The man continued to make fun of the snoring, even suggesting that if the snorer's wife hadn't chided him, that must mean she can snore with the best of them too.

Thurman told the man that there was an extra bed in his room and he could sleep there. Gratefully, the man agreed to this offer. The complaining man went to sleep first, and Thurman settled down for an evening of reading. Thurman said that (you guessed it) soon after, "it began—the most pronounced and heavy snoring I had ever heard in my life."

Thurman had to leave the bedroom and sleep in another part of the suite. When the complaining man woke up and saw Thurman sound asleep, he responded, "Oh no! Don't tell me. I'll never blow my top again about snorers."

Thurman sums this story up by saying, "It is very easy to sit in judgment upon the behavior of others but often difficult to realize that every judgment is a self-judgment. . . . What I condemn in others may be but a reflection of myself in a mirror."[4]

Self-examination, done in a spirit of humility, can curb

much of our judgmentalism. When we focus our attention on our own integrity and inconsistencies, our souls get formed to see with greater precision. To be sure, there is a place for correction and seeking to help someone grow (we'll talk about that in a moment), but order is important.

I think of these words of Abba Joseph, the Desert Father: "How can I pass judgment when I don't know the full truth about myself?"[5] That is what Jesus wants us to see.

To grow in this takes lots of practice. We don't need a seminar to learn how to judge others; it's something we naturally do. Self-examination is hard work. To help with it, let me suggest three questions for reflection:

1. *Where am I failing to live up to a standard I expect from others?* (failure)

2. *How do I currently benefit from the patience and grace of God (and others)?* (forgiveness)

3. *Who in my life can help me see some of my blind spots?* (friendship)

Once the plank in your own eye is removed, the issue we see in a neighbor looks like sawdust. Jesus's point is not that those around us don't have significant issues for which they need guidance and direction, but in light of our self-examination, the issues of others are put into perspective. Judgment of others then comes from a place of humility, not pride.

Learning to Withhold Judgment

How do we become people who follow Jesus's teachings on judgment? Every day, in our interactions with others—in person and on social media—we have plenty of opportunities to practice withholding judgment, but it's easy to slip into cancel culture and gossip. I suggest three things: cultivating the language of "puzzle," resisting hierarchies of sin, and studying the prayer of Examen.

Cultivating the Language of "Puzzle"

In *Emotionally Healthy Relationships,* Pete and Geri Scazzero suggested the phrase "I'm puzzled" to help us reduce judgment. Because human beings are judging machines, we are quick to assume the worst about others, but by adding *puzzle* to our vocabulary, we stop judgments in their tracks. The Scazzeros wrote about puzzles:

- We use them when we don't want to make negative assumptions about people, especially when we don't have all the information.

- Puzzles prevent us from jumping to conclusions and negatively interpreting what is going on around us.

- Puzzles give us an opportunity to slow down and ask questions instead of making judgments.

- *Puzzle* is a loving word.[6]

We have used this language in our congregation for more than two decades and it has helped us navigate many issues.

Let me offer a few scenarios to help you see how puzzle language creates a better way.

Situation #1—You sent an important email to someone one week ago, but they haven't responded yet. Instinctively, you form a negative opinion about this person. Perhaps you think they are avoiding you or that you're not a priority for them. Maybe they're lazy or irresponsible. You tell yourself all kinds of narratives about this person, each one leading to harsh judgment.

What's the alternative? It could be as simple as writing a follow-up email or mentioning your dilemma in person when you see them. You could say something to the effect of, "I sent an email a week ago. I'm puzzled as to why I haven't heard back yet. Could you get back to me at your earliest convenience?" I know how wooden this sounds at first. In fact, you might think this sounds passive-aggressive (depending on your tone, it might), but you're giving someone an opportunity to explain without your jumping to conclusions. It might be the person you reached out to was away on a trip or had a busy week and emails piled up. Either way, you're slowing down to better understand.

Situation #2—You ask your roommate to throw out the trash. When you get home later that day, you see that the trash is still there. Immediately, you judge him in your heart. He's lazy, forgetful, and inconsiderate. When you see him, your words are short and sharp.

What's another way to approach this? When you get home, you see the trash. You take a deep breath, recognizing the force of judgment rising up in you. You send a text message: "Hey, I'm a bit puzzled to see the trash still here. What happened?" Your roommate might respond with a legitimate reason as to why he forgot. Or he might take ownership and apologize and commit to doing better. But the phrase "I'm puzzled" helps you avoid the path of judgment.

Again, this kind of language can feel forced, but the more you use it, the more fruit it will bear. As I said, we've used it in our congregation for decades and it's shaped our culture in positive ways.

Resisting Hierarchies of Sin

Have you ever noticed how someone else's sin usually seems worse than our own? It is very easy to judge another person's weakness according to our strength in that area. However, we are *all* weak in different ways. Humans like to create hierarchies of sin that label some menial and others major.

Self-justification is a powerful impulse; it's our way of maintaining a sense of control. To be sure, not all sins are equal in terms of their impact. There are gradations of sin's effects. A greedy person doesn't have the same impact as a greedy nation. Having an affair causes relational fallout much more than a split-second lustful thought. So yes, sin creates different kinds of consequences, but I want to focus here on the danger of *ranking* sins—usually in a way that vilifies others and excuses ourselves—and how Jesus's kingdom operates on an entirely different paradigm.

Creating hierarchies is explicitly rejected by Jesus, as seen in his scathing rebuke of religious leaders who prioritize obedience in some areas and neglect others. He says,

Woe to you, teachers of the law and Pharisees, you hypocrites! You give a tenth of your spices—mint, dill and cumin. But you have neglected the more important matters of the law—justice, mercy and faithfulness. You should have practiced the latter, without neglecting the former. (Matthew 23:23)

In this exchange, Jesus rejects the shortsighted approach of the religious leaders, which was scrupulous on minutiae and negligent on weightier matters. In his kindness, he redirects us from this sort of lopsided spirituality, even if his doing so stings on the front end. To walk the narrow path means releasing any system that excuses our own sin by magnifying the sin of others. To see ourselves honestly is the only path to freedom. Along with the apostle Paul, we confess, "I'm the chief among sinners" (see 1 Timothy 1:15).

In daily life, this means that we must be on guard against the "sin lists" we have created. These lists, oriented around our personal vendettas, reveal our view of God and what we think he cares about. You might fixate on sexual ethics, indifference toward the poor, vitriol toward political opponents, or some other issue. There are times for prophetic protest, but first and foremost, Jesus invites us to examine our own hearts and acknowledge the sin residing there.

Studying the Prayer of Examen

If you know me, you know I love the prayer of Examen, a spiritual practice that helps me prayerfully review my day. In some traditions, this pause-and-reflect moment happens at midday and before retiring for the night. It's an approach to spirituality that centers God's presence and helps us live a steady life of confession and repentance (two things that confront judgmentalism).

Looking back over the day can be difficult, especially when we've been impatient or inconsistent, but it gives us an opportunity to receive grace for our shortcomings, and strength for the day ahead. When I practice the Examen, I use these four questions:

1. *Did I see anyone through the eyes of Christ's love today?*

2. *Did I bring my anxious thoughts before God in prayer?*

3. *Was I present to God's presence in silence?*

4. *Is there any sin I must confess and request God's forgiveness for?*

Practicing this simple prayer, I've learned that when I search my own heart, I have less time to find fault in others.

Withholding judgment is part of the narrow path of Jesus, and few choose it. Why? Because it reminds us there is Someone who holds ultimate judgment. When we choose self-examination over judging, we confess with our lives that we don't see as God does. Therefore, in humility, we surrender our verdicts to the One who judges righteously.

It's common for many people to view the judgment of God as bad news. But in Christ, we see that this is the best news in the world. Unlike that of humans, God's judgment is entirely accurate, loving, and wise. God is steadfast against evil. He is compassionate beyond measure. His judgment is always in the context of grace. I don't know exactly how he will judge the world in the fullness of his wisdom, but as I look at Jesus, I can only conclude that his judgment will be rooted in the kind of love that heals and redeems. And because we are not privy to the wise ways of God, we are called to entrust our lives (and the lives of others) to his perfect character.

OUR DECISIONS

"Pastor Rich, no offense, but life is hard and busy as it is. Now you want me to mysteriously discover God's will for my life? I have no idea how to do that."

This was the honest feedback I received from a congregant facing a very challenging life situation. I was grateful for her words, as I can slip into Christian clichés rather quickly, exhorting the people I pastor to "pursue God's will." She helped me step back and assess this common spiritual question: *What is the will of God for my life, and how do I discover it?*

When we talk about God's will, we often think in terms of *decisions.* For example, *What does God want me to do in this situation?* Perhaps you're single, weighing the pros and cons of dating. Maybe you're trying to decide if you should transition from a company you've been with for fifteen years. Maybe your parents are getting older, so you're considering whether or not to have them move in with you.

Sometimes we're afraid we've missed God's will. A wrong decision here, an impulsive move there, and we wonder if life has careened off the tracks. We sense we've strayed from God's path, but it's unclear what the next step is. As Martin Luther King, Jr., said in his final sermon, "I just want to do God's will."[1] That's what we all want. But is it possible?

Jesus's answer is a resounding yes! His will is not a maze to navigate—one wrong turn and we're disqualified. Life with Jesus is so much better than that. The narrow path is not a trick; it's an invitation to know and love God.

The Hiddenness of our Hearts

As Jesus nears the end of the Sermon on the Mount, he reiterates something he's emphasized throughout: The depths of our hearts are seen by God. This all-seeing God calls us to a life of interior examination. A life that recognizes the possibility—or, rather, the inevitability—of self-deception. Jesus knows that our deeds can seem righteous, with rotten motives underneath. Nowhere in his sermon does this come to light more terrifyingly than here:

> Not everyone who says to me, "Lord, Lord," will enter the kingdom of heaven, but only the one who does the will of my Father who is in heaven. Many will say to me on that day, "Lord, Lord, did we not prophesy in your name and in your name drive out demons

and in your name perform many miracles?" Then I will tell them plainly, "I never knew you. Away from me, you evildoers!" (Matthew 7:21–23)

When I read these words, I'm jolted by his directness. At the heart of this warning, there is grace. Jesus loves us too much to play games with the truth. He invites us into a life of knowing God, not just knowing *about* God. A life of presence, not posturing. A life of *being with* God, not simply *doing things for* him. Jesus is not interested in a spirituality that separates motive from mission. He calls us to congruence—to a life unfractured and secure.

The problem is, it's easy to do religious things for the wrong reasons. Just prior to this passage, Jesus warns about "wolves" who pose as sheep—in other words, false prophets who act like disciples but deceive the church. For various reasons, people come into our lives with deceitful motives. They are people who live for themselves. People looking for power and prestige who devour anyone who stands in their way.

What makes them menacing is their so-called God-talk and God-life. They go to church every Sunday, volunteer at food banks, and hang Bible verses on their walls. C. S. Lewis wrote, "If the Divine call does not make us better, it will make us very much worse. *Of all bad men religious bad men are the worst.* Of all created beings the wickedest is one who originally stood in the immediate presence of God."[2] Yikes.

The broad path teems with wolves. So how do we avoid them, and even more poignantly, how do we avoid becoming one? Jesus doesn't want to say, "I never knew you," any more than you want to hear him say it. Ask this fundamental question: *Am I on a journey to really know Jesus, or have I been using him for my own benefit?*

Judgment Day

Jesus makes it clear that good works alone do not please him *unless* they flow from a life of attentiveness to his will. Whew. Take a deep breath.

If the idea of the Day of Judgment (which Jesus is describing here) makes you squirm, I'm with you. When I hear this topic, I instantly picture angry, finger-pointing people on the street corner. I've always found it curious that the loudest voices appealing to God's judgment tend to be people who have a finely curated catalog of sins that need to be punished. But here, the judgment is not for hungover partiers slumped over on the couch; it's for religious, have-it-all-together types whom everyone perceives as holy.

The Day of Judgment that Jesus alludes to speaks to the final sorting of God. While we are never to assume how God will ultimately fulfill his values of love and justice, we are made to live under the reality of that coming day. For modern ears, this can sound spiritually manipulative and coercive.

Maybe you're thinking, *God's judgment often sounds eerily similar to the projections of preachers and fearful religious types.* Perhaps you reject any notion whatsoever of being subjected to judgment. But again, listen closely to Jesus here. Yes, God will judge the world, but the emphasis here is placed on those who have represented him without truly knowing him. He's naming the counterfeit so you don't get conned into spiritual blindness.

Powerful Mission, Problematic Motive

Jesus is warning those who have good theology. The people being judged in Jesus's telling of the Day of Judgment are orthodox on paper. They are card-carrying members of the faith. They address Jesus as Lord. They have mentally assented to the unique status of Jesus. Their theological *i*'s and *t*'s are dotted and crossed. What we learn is a hard but necessary lesson: Having knowledge—even saving knowledge—doesn't mean you know Jesus.

One of the greatest points of spiritual self-deception is believing that having knowledge is the goal of the Christian life. James said it this way to a group of local Christians: "You believe that there is one God. Good! Even the demons believe that—and shudder" (James 2:19). He says that demons have good theology *and* feel the weight of it, but it makes no difference to them. That concept is important for people who place great emphasis on believing the "right" things but do not carry them out in the way they live.

Jesus also addresses the motives of these spiritually elite people. Yes, they are helping people—even in profound ways, like casting out demons or healing people from diseases—but they don't *know* him. In Scripture, the word *know* denotes profound intimacy. A mutual exchange of life. Jesus tells them, "I never knew you" (Matthew 7:23).

You can know *about* Taylor Swift or LeBron James. You can sing every song by heart and articulate every statistic by memory. But if you randomly show up where they live, saying, "I love you. Can I stay awhile?" you'll be . . . swiftly arrested. In the same way, it's possible to know *about* God without cultivating a deep friendship with him.

In his kingdom, mission matters, but so does motive. Everything we do must flow from love of God and neighbor, as Paul says in 1 Corinthians 13:

> If I speak in the tongues of men or of angels, but do not have love, I am only a resounding gong or a clanging cymbal. If I have the gift of prophecy and can fathom all mysteries and all knowledge, and if I have a faith that can move mountains, but do not have love, I am nothing. If I give all I possess to the poor and give over my body to hardship that I may boast, but do not have love, I gain nothing. (verses 1–3)

As a leader, I'm constantly trying to sift my motives through those words. In his book *Theology as a Way of Life,* Adam Neder named an uncomfortable truth, especially for those who make a living off "God-talk":

> Consider, for example, how easily we forget that every Christian leader profits off of Jesus Christ's suffering and death. He gets crucified and we get paid. That's the arrangement. Jesus suffers and we cash in. If you teach the Christian faith and that does not unsettle you, you are not thinking straight.[3]

This warning—that motives get mixed even when we're trying to serve God—isn't just for clergy. We can volunteer at church because we want to be part of the inner circle of leadership. We can be generous for important causes in order to garner praise. We can do good things for *our* glory, not God's.

That is why some people *think* they're doing the will of

God even when they're not. Miracles. Casting out demons. Serving. Amazingly, amid all this activity, they forget the most important thing: to love him. Jesus's warning is not meant to create dread; instead, it leads us to discernment and is a clarion call to examine our decisions today. Are we doing our wills, someone else's, or God's?

Discovering and Doing God's Will

Discovering God's will—and actually doing it—is one of the great tasks of following the narrow path of Jesus that leads to a satisfying life. It takes discernment, which doesn't come naturally for most of us. I've found that the approaches I've used in making decisions over the course of my life fall into three categories.

First, **I have been someone who always discerns but never decides.** I mull over the options again and again, too afraid to make a decision. Beneath the surface of my indecision is usually some emotional baggage that I haven't worked through. For example, as a leader, I can gather all the information I need regarding a particular initiative but, because of my fear of failure, analyze my way to inactivity. The baggage of previous failures can imprison me if I'm not careful.

On the flip side, **I have been someone who frequently decides without discerning.** This is the exact mistake of those to whom Jesus says, "I never knew you" (Matthew 7:23). Sometimes I'm so fixated on what I want that I shoot from the hip instead of seeking God.

Occasionally, by God's grace, **I make decisions from a place of discernment.** When we decided to move into a different neighborhood in New York, my initial impulse was to look for the best financial deal. Of course, that was part of the process, but Rosie and I took the time to prayerfully think through values such as proximity to people in our congregation and the desire to be more hospitable. As a leader, I've also had to discern how to address sensitive matters (such as racism, politics, and sexuality). Naturally, discerning well doesn't mean the discussion always goes well! However, it is an area of life I'm growing in.

To reassure you, the people being judged by Jesus in Matthew 7 have not made just a few bad decisions. We all will make mistakes. The problem is, throughout their *entire lives*, they never stopped to consider God's will. Jesus tells them, "I *never* knew you." This lack of reflection snowballed into lives of religious activity apart from Jesus. And once we are sliding down that steep hill, it's hard to stop.

Doing God's will necessitates *knowing* his will. How do we do that? Here are four components to consider:

1. Desire it.

2. Search the Scriptures.

3. Listen to your heart.

4. Pursue community wisdom.

Let's briefly walk through each of these.

Desire God's Will

In Psalm 40:8, David wrote, "I desire to do your will, my God; your law is within my heart." Note what he didn't say: "I delight to *think* about your will" or "I delight to *consider* your will." Nor does he say, "I delight to *know* your will."

He desires to *do* it. God's will should be obeyed, not merely considered. That is why Jesus teaches us to pray, "Your kingdom come, your will be *done*" (Matthew 6:10).

David knows deep down in his soul that God's will is good and worthy of being carried out. Admittedly, I sometimes struggle to relate. To pray, "God's will be done," has been very challenging for me over the years. Beneath my reticence has been a lurking suspicion that God wants me to be miserable. And why would I desire greater misery? I've been a Knicks fan all my life. That should be enough.

Do you ever wonder if following Jesus is worth it? Do you suspect that his narrow path might steal your freedom? You're not alone.

If there's one truth that's helped me, it's this: God is like Jesus.

When I behold Jesus in the Scriptures, I see the full revelation of who God is. I encourage you to see Jesus at work in the gospel stories. Take note of the people he offers compassion to. Meditate on his penchant for forgiveness. Watch whom he touches and welcomes and whom he rebukes. Contemplate his self-giving love, his conquering of death, his defeat of the powers, his abundant care. When our images of God are healed, we can desire his will, trusting that it is good.

I came across a liturgy that helped me feel the force of this truth. "A Bedtime Blessing of Gospel Love" is a series of questions that a parent can recite with their little one before turning out the lights. I like this prayer because it helps form a particular image of God in children from a young age. Children are very impressionable, so knowing early on that his character is rooted in goodness and love establishes a strong foundation to trust in his will. Read these beautiful words:

Parent: Do you see my eyes?

Child: Yes.

Parent: Can you see that I see your eyes?

Child: Yes.

Parent: Do you know that I love you?

Child: Yes.

Parent: Do you know that I love you no matter what good things you do?

Child: Yes.

Parent: Do you know that I love you no matter what bad things you do?

Child: Yes.

Parent: Who else loves you like that?

Child: God does.

Parent: Even more than me?

Child: Yes.

Parent: Rest in that love.[4]

I did this with my four-year-old son, Nathan. When I got to the part that asks, "Who else loves you like that?" he responded, "Santa." Obviously, I still have work to do.

Here's the point: Jesus gives us a vision of God's goodness that forms us to obey not from a forced sense of duty but from a place of delight and desire. To desire God's will is to open ourselves to the countercultural way of Jesus's narrow path. And although it is difficult, it produces the lives we long for.

Desiring God's will is a grace of the Spirit. Through the

years, I have learned to pray, "Lord, grant me the desire to know and do your will. And when that desire is not there, grant me the discipline to seek you." There are no easy steps to obtaining desire. But as we open ourselves to Jesus, especially in prayer and meditating on Scripture, the Spirit can do in us what we can't do for ourselves.

Search the Scriptures

To discern God's will, we must saturate ourselves in the wisdom of the Holy Scriptures. While the Bible can be a challenging and demanding book to read, in its pages we learn the value system of God's kingdom. Of course, we will not find the answers to every question (for example, *Should I go to this college or that one?* or *Should I retire or keep working?*). However, Scripture provides the principles and wisdom we need. Keep in mind, to discern God's will through the Bible requires a steady, slow, and inquisitive approach (in conversation with others) to pay attention to aspects of God's will that can easily be overlooked.

Listen to Your Heart

I've heard for many years that we can't trust our hearts. There's usually a Bible verse to support this claim, such as, "The heart is deceitful above all things and beyond cure. Who can understand it?" (Jeremiah 17:9). Many people have taken this verse to mean that our heart's desires are to be viewed with great suspicion. But there's another verse that needs to be considered. The prophet Ezekiel prophesied of a day when God "will give you a new heart and put a new spirit in you; I will remove from you your heart of stone and give you a heart of flesh" (Ezekiel 36:26).

Every time someone trusts in Jesus and is filled with the Holy Spirit, that promise is fulfilled. If we follow Jesus, we can listen discerningly to our hearts, trusting the presence of the Spirit to guide us.

It's easy to believe that the desires of our hearts must be set aside so we can do God's will. But it's crucial to know that God works *through our hearts.* Paul said it this way to the church in Philippi: "It is God who works in you *to will* and to act in order to fulfill his good purpose" (Philippians 2:13).

Not every desire we have is an obstacle to God's will. Although some desires may be inconsistent with God's heart for us, we should listen to our hearts, with the help of the Holy Spirit, as we seek to discover God's will.

That said, as we follow our Spirit-shaped hearts, it's always wise to test those thoughts among trusted Christians who know and love us. That is the final—and very important—aspect of discerning God's will that's helped me.

Pursue Community Wisdom

One of my favorite passages of Scripture is found in the book of Acts. The church was at a significant point in its history, discerning how to integrate Gentile and Jewish believers under the kingship of Jesus. That meant the leadership needed to assess the degree to which Gentiles would be subject to Jewish norms and customs. The apostles and elders concluded, "It seemed good to the Holy Spirit and to us" (15:28). And to us. Those three words remind us that God's wisdom and guidance is not always mysterious. In fact, it's readily available to us, but discovering it often requires community input and discernment. When facing a decision, clarity comes when we pray and discuss it with others who seek God alongside us.

At one point in our lives, with two small children, the task of parenting and leading a church became overwhelming for Rosie and me. We began to have conversations with friends and family members to help us think through practical ways to navigate that season. After a series of conversations, it became apparent that moving into my in-laws' home for two years was necessary to help us survive the emotional wear and tear we were experiencing. To be honest, I was ashamed to make this move because it felt like a giant step backward. Here I was, leading a large, well-known congregation in New York City, and I was moving in with my in-laws. After more processing, our community of friends encouraged and reframed the messages I was carrying within. They helped me see the decision as life-giving, not lame. That is the gift of community wisdom.

As we near the end of this chapter, you might still feel intimidated by Jesus's warning. You might be worried that someday you'll hear him say, "I never knew you." You might be wondering, *What does God really want from me?* That question may sound strange or defensive, but it's meant to be honest. Clearly, obedience matters to Jesus, and yet, we are saved by grace. Let's consider how this all fits together, so we can be confident (not terrified) about doing God's will.

Doing God's Will

Are we saved by grace or by works? I used to get very worked up whenever I heard this polarizing question. I can't tell you how many passionate (and unhealthy) arguments I've had with people about this. (Some of you might feel your own passion rising within you as you read these words.) It's impossible to satisfy your theological convictions and questions in a few paragraphs, but I'll tell you how I've emotionally moved on from this age-old point of division: I simply read the Bible on its own terms (which emphasizes *both* works and grace) and have learned to hold those seemingly conflicting ideas in tension.

To put it plainly, we are saved through Jesus Christ alone. I believe that he is the only Savior of the world. In his life, death, resurrection, and enthronement, he has been declared Lord. In him, we are invited into a salvation project that seamlessly holds together our believing and doing.

Jesus says that the only ones who will see the kingdom of God are those who do the will of the Father. That is quite a problematic statement for those who carry an easy-believism approach to faith—a view that sees salvation as a onetime act with little bearing on one's subsequent lifestyle. It sees heaven—rather than submission to the rule of Jesus—as the aim. It focuses on what can be received but avoids the hard reality of taking up one's cross. This kind of faith is reductionistic, viewing Jesus's narrow way as optional, not demanded. A path to secure our eternal future, but not a road to follow here and now.

Jesus is clear: Entrance to the kingdom is found in *doing*. This does not mean salvation is a reward for our good behavior, but in the mind of Jesus (and later the apostle Paul), salvation is a gift that always creates a generous and concrete response.

I pastor a congregation where more than seventy-five nations are represented. Many congregants are first-generation immigrants. Something I've learned in my context is that giving gifts often creates a cycle of gift giving. That is how the rich theological word *grace* should be understood.

I remember purchasing a T-shirt I saw for an older East Asian congregant after the two of us had a meaningful conversation. One week later, the congregant dropped off a beautiful journal and book to the church office. At first I wondered if the congregant misunderstood that the shirt was a gift and I didn't need anything in return. However, I made a cultural discovery: His gift wasn't given out of guilt but grace.

The gift of salvation is not a one-way transaction; it unlocks a process of mutual self-giving. Through Christ, we are declared righteous through faith. Faith then creates a new movement where we, in turn, do the will of the Father in heaven. In the words of James, "What good is it, my brothers and sisters, if someone claims to have faith but has no deeds? Can such faith save them?" (James 2:14). The answer is no.

If faith makes no practical difference in the way we live, there's a disconnect. The biggest hindrance to the gospel is not atheism or some other religion; it's when Christian faith is expressed in name only. The quality of our faith is not in what we *claim* to believe; rather, it flows from our intimate communion with God that is expressed in love for others, in accordance with the Father's will.

Jesus invites you onto the narrow path, where obedience is delight, not drudgery. He will lead you step-by-step so you don't have to fret about "finding" God's will. He will love you when you stumble, so rest assured he is for you.

12

OUR ENEMIES

Mark Twain once quipped, "It ain't the parts of the Bible that I can't understand that bother me, it's the parts that I do understand."

When it comes to Jesus's word on loving our enemies, Twain's quote resonates. I'm bothered by this teaching of Jesus. It might be the most difficult of all his sayings. And it might be the most important, especially in our divided world.

Humanity is trained to see enemies in two primary ways: They should be avoided at any cost, or they should be destroyed by any means. However, on the narrow path, we are called to seek the good of our enemies. Ouch.

Now, some of you might be thinking, *I don't really have enemies. Sure, that co-worker annoys me. The neighbor two houses down yelled at me once. Things with my in-laws can be tense . . . but they're not my enemies!* Before you read on to the next chapter, allow me to challenge this assumption.

On one level, an enemy is a person or group who opposes another person or group with the intent to harm them—in word or deed. I remember searching for a video on YouTube and, in the process, was surprised to see a video of someone who used to attend my congregation saying hurtful things about me. After my initial shock, I immediately categorized that guy as an enemy.

But I also would like to suggest—more broadly—that an enemy is anyone you have a hard time loving. Perhaps this is an enemy with a lowercase *e*. You might not have an enemy in the classical sense, but for our purposes here, an enemy is someone you are against or someone who is against you.

An enemy can be the boss who fired you. A husband who cheated on you. Someone who said something hurtful or took advantage of you. An enemy can be someone who just annoys you, or they can be a certain ethnic group or political party. Your enemy can be someone who hurt someone you love. Even if you don't have an enemy now, chances are that you will have one sooner or later.

Jesus has instructions for us about how we think about and treat these people. Buckle up: He says to *love them and pray for them*. This isn't a command to feign friendliness. For the follower of Jesus, it's a matter of obedience and formation. We love and pray for enemies not because it feels good to do so but because our Lord calls us to be different from the world.

The Right Kind of Enemy

There are some reading this who see many people as their enemies, so it's worthwhile to pause here and clarify: Do you have enemies because you're following Jesus on the narrow path, or is it because you're irresponsibly hurting others in his name? As an example, I remember one of my first jobs as a new Christian. I debated co-workers, insulted their thinking regarding religion, and was passive-aggressive. Not surprisingly, I created some enemies. When they, in turn, spoke to me sarcastically or ridiculed my faith, I concluded I was being faithful to Jesus. That is the wrong kind of enemy-making. It requires three simple missteps:

1. Act like a jerk in the name of Jesus.
2. Notice the negative reactions of people around you.
3. Claim faithfulness to Jesus. (Religious persecution is a favorite outcry.)

So, do we have the same kind of enemies Jesus did? That's the question. The enemies we have as followers of Jesus reveal whether we're living like him or not. The right kind of enemies (as strange as that sounds) are those who disparage us because we have an otherworldly love and care for the powerless. It seems to me that Christians often make the "wrong kind" of enemies because of our refusal to love well.

Love for Enemies

Jesus says, "You have heard that it was said, 'Love your neighbor and hate your enemy.' But I tell you, love your enemies and pray for those who persecute you, that you may be children of your Father in heaven" (Matthew 5:43–45).

Although the Old Testament doesn't instruct the people

of God to literally hate their enemy, that sentiment was prevalent and widely accepted. Jesus confronts the cultural atmosphere that made it permissible to treat supposed enemies with abject disregard.

This "Hate your neighbor" doctrine is alive and well in every generation. In the words of Anne Lamott's priest friend Tom, "You can safely assume you've created God in your own image when it turns out that God hates all the same people you do."[1]

Jesus calls his followers away from enemy hate into enemy love. Before you close this book in frustration, let's explore what it means to love enemies.

What Is Love?

When it comes to defining and embodying love, look to Jesus—especially how he engages with people who wish him harm.

It's easy to believe that loving enemies means serving as a doormat. Turn the other cheek, right? It's common to assume that enemy love requires positive feelings toward those who maliciously oppose us. Let's observe Jesus's interactions in the Gospels to get a comprehensive perspective.

Prayer

First, let's note one of the primary ways Jesus invites us to love our enemies: to pray for them. Our prayers have ways of shaping our presence in the world. Some cynics might retort, "I pray for my enemies . . . prayers for their demise!" Look, I get it. I've done the same, and with good biblical precedent. Just read some of the imprecatory psalms—that is, songs in the Bible that beg God to bring calamity on enemies! Here are some examples:

> Break the arm of the wicked man;
>> call the evildoer to account for
>>> his wickedness
>> that would not otherwise be found out.
>> (10:15)

> May what you have stored up for the wicked
>> fill their bellies;
>> may their children gorge themselves on it,
>> and may there be leftovers for their little
>>> ones. (17:14)

> Since they hid their net for me without cause
>> and without cause dug a pit for me,
> may ruin overtake them by surprise—
>> may the net they hid entangle them,
>> may they fall into the pit, to their ruin.
>> (35:7–8)

You get the point.

It's normal for our prayers to be raw and filled with rage and grief. This grounds us in reality and opens us to God's presence. If you never pray your anger, it bottles up inside and becomes dangerous. Jesus can handle—even invites—your honest prayers.

That said, even though the imprecatory psalms are *re-*

corded in Scripture, they're not *recommended* as a way of life. Jesus calls us to pray *for* our enemies. In prayer, we give ourselves space to be formed by the Holy Spirit. This formation comes gradually, not instantly.

Some years ago, a Benedictine monk visited our church. He gave a lecture on forgiveness and shared this prayer for our enemies:

> May you be happy. May you be free.
> May you be loving. May you be loved.
> May you know the fulfillment of what God has
>   planned for you.
> May you experience God's deep, profound love
>   for you.
> May you receive and grow in the fullness of the
>   graces Jesus has won for you.
> May Jesus Christ be formed in you.
> May you know His peace that passes all under-
>   standing.
> May all good things be yours.
> May Jesus's joy be in you, and may that joy be
>   complete.
> May you know the Lord in all His goodness and
>   compassion.
> May you be protected from the evil one amid
>   every temptation that comes your way.
> May the Holy Spirit fill and permeate your entire
>   being.
> May you see His glory.
> May you be forgiven of every sin.
> I forgive you (or will try to forgive you) of every
>   wound and hurt with all my heart.

> May God's goodness and mercy follow you all
> the days of your life.[2]

When I first read this prayer, I laughed. It was cynical laughter. Years later, I realized that this is the narrow path of Jesus, which is foolishness to the world.

Truth-Telling

Let us now focus on an aspect of enemy love that you might enjoy a bit more (I sure do), but my eagerness must be tempered. When I observe Jesus, the embodiment of perfect love, I notice that he wasn't always nice. Niceness is not a fruit of the Holy Spirit.

Jesus spoke the truth in love and in ways that corresponded to reality. Take a look at his words to the religious leaders:

> Woe to you, teachers of the law and Pharisees, you hypocrites! You shut the door of the kingdom of heaven in people's faces. You yourselves do not enter, nor will you let those enter who are trying to. (Matthew 23:13)

Or my favorite,

> You snakes! You brood of vipers! How will you escape being condemned to hell? (verse 33)

We must conclude that Jesus said these either in love or in sin. When we examine the rest of Scripture, it's clear that, although hard to read, these words are an expression of love. This is one of the ways Jesus loved his enemies: by telling them the truth.

But a word of caution here. It's common for people to want to flip tables because Jesus did or call their enemies "snakes" like he did. When Jesus offered these words, he had love, compassion, and justice in mind. He was naming the hypocrisy of religious leaders and the spiritual burdens they placed on the backs of people in the name of God. Jesus's words were proportionate to the systemic sin of the leaders.

To reiterate a quote from Dietrich Bonhoeffer, "Truth just for oneself, truth spoken in enmity and hate is not truth but a lie, for truth brings us into God's presence, and God is love. Truth is either the clarity of love, or it is nothing."[3]

That is why prayer must be connected to truth-telling, especially when we are talking about enemies. In telling the truth to those we perceive as enemies, we hope to free them from the bondage of their own hypocrisy, as well as the hurt they pour out on others.

The gospel is good news for the burdened and the burdener. For the powerless and the powerful. Both are liberated in different ways. The burdened are raised up from destructive treatment, the burdener from the harm they inflict on others and themselves. In the words of American writer James Baldwin, "One cannot deny the humanity of another without diminishing one's own."[4]

To speak truth—especially in a public manner—is to subject ourselves to criticism. The best we can do is prayerfully and humbly examine our motivations, weigh our words, and speak with courage. When we do, whether others see it or not, we are loving our enemies.

Compassion

Jesus also loves his enemies through compassion—seen most profoundly on the cross, where he prays, "Father, forgive them, for they do not know what they are doing" (Luke 23:34). What a beautiful, confounding display of love. Jesus knows the harmful messages his murderers carry. He knows the violence that corrupts their lives. He knows the dehumanizing forces filling their hearts. He knows they are oppressed by a larger, insidious power. Jesus knows that those who fail to love are bent low under the crushing weight of sin. With tears in his eyes, he pronounces a word of compassion.

He knows their stories. He is grieved by their bondage. He understands the prison they find themselves in. In response, he pours out forgiveness.

To love our enemies is to acknowledge the painful truth that their words and deeds usually emerge from a place that needs healing. Where the world sees only enemies, the narrow path of Jesus makes space for the larger stories of their lives.

I try to do this, with varying degrees of success. When someone says something hurtful, my first response is to fight back. In some of my better moments, I've been able to reflect on that moment. I ask, *What might be going on in that person to make them say such a thing?* I try to ask the same question when observing public figures, especially politicians. I try to imagine the fear they carry that leads to demonization and fearmongering. I try to recognize the anxiety they might feel, or relate to their longing for power and influence (desires I battle daily).

To practice this incarnational curiosity is not to excuse,

minimize, or ignore the decisions people make, especially when they harm others. Instead, it means engaging with them from a deeper place of love. This love can't be mustered by human strength; it comes only from following Jesus in the power of the Spirit.

In the Old Testament, when God tells Jonah to preach repentance to his enemies, he refuses. Why? Because he suspects God will offer them grace! He takes a ship in the opposite direction of where God tells him to go. You know the story—the storm, the big fish, and, finally, Jonah preaches a seemingly straightforward sermon to the people, and shockingly, they repent!

The next scene is staggering. Jonah might be the only preacher who gets upset when the congregation actually repents and turns to God!

Jonah despises the people of Nineveh (and for good reason), yet the last verse in the book gives us a glimpse into the heart of God:

> Should I not have concern for the great city of Nineveh, in which there are more than a hundred and twenty thousand people who cannot tell their right hand from their left—and also many animals? (Jonah 4:11)

God sees the moral backwardness of the Ninevites. He acknowledges the state of their lostness. And this recognition leads to compassion.

This is the compassion God expects from Jonah. And from you and me.

One of the major themes of the book of Jonah is God's kindness to the Ninevites. But the underlying message is far more jolting. Besides helping the Ninevites, God is trying to save Jonah the prophet from his judgmentalism, his hard heart, his finger-pointing, and his self-righteousness.

The best measure of spiritual maturity is not how much you know about God but how much you imitate his love toward enemies. There is no narrower path than this. Along this way, difficult as it is at times, lies the deepest satisfaction a soul can ever know. Jesus invites you and me to follow him down the narrow path.

PRACTICING OBEDIENCE

I want to end our journey with one word: *obedience*. (I know you were probably hoping for something more up-lifting, but please stick with me.) It's not a word many people like, except, well, dog owners, parents of small kids, and power-hungry people. (I'm sure there's a Venn diagram for this.)

Obedience gets a bad rap. Some see it through the lens of oppression. But in the kingdom of Jesus, it's the secret to the life that truly satisfies our souls.

By the end of the Sermon on the Mount, his magisterial sermon, Jesus has touched on what constitutes a blessed life. He's shown the importance of integrity and simple speech. He's invited us into the confounding way of subversive love. He's taught us about money, prayer, and how to deal with anxiety. He's guided us into lives free of judgment and helped us see the necessity of discernment. Oh, and he's challenged us to pray for our enemies. Whew, that's a lot.

But he's not done.

Jesus understands something about the human condition: that hearing truth means nothing if it's not actively practiced. To hear truth without steady implementation is to deceive ourselves into thinking that knowledge equals maturity.

But knowledge is not enough. Hearing truth is not enough. It's for this reason the apostle James said, "Do not merely listen to the word, and so deceive yourselves. Do what it says" (James 1:22). Why is listening without action deceptive? It's because as we listen, we feel like we're being formed by what we hear. I know plenty of people—myself included—who can quote chapter and verse but haven't been personally changed by that truth.

How do we avoid this trap? For Jesus, the answer is found in *practice*. Until there is a reordering of our lives, we will return to our old ways.

Practice

In the final portion of his sermon, Jesus makes an important distinction: A life built on a strong foundation is available to the one who hears his teachings *and puts them into practice*. Conversely, those who listen without obeying build their lives on a shaky, flimsy foundation.

Read Jesus's words slowly: "*Everyone who hears these words of mine and does not put them into practice* is like a foolish man who built his house on sand" (Matthew 7:26).

Jesus is most concerned with his followers *living out* the life-transforming teaching he offers.

Obedience to Jesus is found in practicing his teachings. Jesus says that the one who hears and puts what he instructs into practice is the one who builds a life on a firm foundation. (Note: He doesn't say, "Practices perfectly.") In the same way that we all have habits—ways of ordering life through subconscious, repeated behavior—we are called to build ones that propel us down the narrow path.

Our habits either place us on the path of Jesus's kingdom or pull us away from it. Practices form habits. Habits order our lives. The practices we repeat reveal what we love—or what we are enslaved to. The question is, how do we build new habits so Jesus's teachings become the primary source of our decisions and relationships?

It is common for people to talk about a churchgoing person as a *practicing Christian*. This kind of language presupposes that one can be a Christian without practicing the way of Jesus.

Similar to how a basketball player forms muscle memory to shoot the ball through a hoop at a high rate of efficiency, the teachings of Jesus are lived out through rhythms and routines. These habits don't just come as we read about their importance. (I don't brush my teeth in the morning and before bed because I've read about it but because I've cultivated this routine.) The habits we form are shaping our lives. Unless there is a reappraisal of our daily, weekly, monthly, and annual practices, we will only hear the word, not do it.

For the remainder of this book, I'll focus on six simple practices that will help you live into everything we've covered.

#1 Meditate on Jesus's Teachings

New habits are not just built by gathering information. Cognitively, I know eating too many glazed doughnuts is bad for my health, but, alas, I struggle to let that wisdom guide my behavior. To be transformed, we need meditation, not just information.

Meditation is not simply about filling your mind with Bible verses. In fact, the broad path is filled with people who have a lot of scriptures in their heads. Meditation can include memorization, but it's much more. Meditation is the spiritual practice of patiently allowing the truth of Scripture to reorient the way you engage the world. It's not a practice for the so-called spiritually elite; rather, it's about slowly chewing God's Word until it penetrates your heart.

I have made it a practice over many years to meditate on the teachings of Jesus, especially the Sermon on the Mount. I will never plumb the depths of its wisdom or master how to apply it in my life. Still, as I've saturated myself in these words, something has happened to me: I live haunted (in the best sense of the word) by the way of Jesus.

For example, meditating on Jesus's words of enemy love has jolted me when I've wanted to pour out wrath on those I don't like. When I meditate on the teachings of Jesus, I'm not just trying to recall his words; I'm rehearsing them over and over, giving the Holy Spirit ample room to expand my heart. Fixing my attention on his call to not worry has soothed my soul in times of deep anxiety. Sometimes meditation comes in the form of writing out his words in a journal, listening for God's particular invitation to receive peace in a moment of fear.

Pondering his categories of blessedness has helped me

assess what's most important when I'm tempted to reach for more possessions. As I set my heart on the narrow path of Jesus's teachings, I'm more aware of my sin. But, praise God, I'm also more aware of his grace for weak sinners like me.

Reading through the Sermon on the Mount two to three times a month might be a great place to start for you. Meditating and journaling on the Beatitudes can recalibrate your soul. As you give yourself to internalizing and embodying his teachings, the Spirit will work through you to see those words lived out.

Jesus himself models what it looks like to meditate on the Holy Scriptures. When he is tempted in the wilderness, Scripture flows from his lips. When he is challenged by religious leaders, Scripture flows from his lips. Even in his lowest moment, while being crucified, Scripture flows from his lips. To live like Jesus, we must internalize God's Word to the point that, in every circumstance, it pours out of us.

#2 Hunger and Thirst for Righteousness

I know what it's like to talk a good game about pursuing righteousness, especially social righteousness, but not rearrange my life to embody it. That is one of the great dangers of hearing Jesus's words without practicing them.

How is God inviting you to serve those in your community? Perhaps you could provide resources and relationship to those who are economically disenfranchised. It might look like advocating for the vulnerable. Maybe you're called to join (or start) a local community board to represent families in your neighborhood. Perhaps God is calling you to change policies that harm those people the world tends to overlook. But hungering and thirsting for righteousness can show up in many other ways too.

It can be practiced by leading a Bible study with high school students, focusing on God's heart for the vulnerable, followed by a specific call to action. It can be embodied through acts of hospitality toward those in your community who are overlooked during the holidays. It can be expressed by serving as part of your child's parent-teacher association, especially if there are significant gaps. It can be through fundraising to lighten the burden for families in financial peril. You see, practicing righteousness, or justice, doesn't always require a protest march or social media post. The underlying questions are, where is there pain, sin, or need around you? How is Jesus inviting you to respond?

#3 Speak Truthfully (Yes and No)

The practice of examining our level of truth-telling is another important act of discipleship. We would do well to spend time reflecting on questions like these:

- *Where have I been spinning the truth?*

- *Why do I have a hard time being honest with [person's name]?*

- *Why do I feel a need to say yes when I really mean no?*

- *When have I recently been intentionally vague about a matter? What might be beneath this?*

- *When have I gone back on my word to do something? What is contributing to this gap in integrity?*

#4 Pray for Enemies

Many followers of Jesus feel guilty naming the enemies we have in our hearts. Some of the enemies we have are those who have hurt us; others are people we just have a hard time loving. I remember having a conversation with dear friends and we went around the room naming the people we have a hard time loving. It was quite freeing to know that we all had someone on our minds. We also used that time to pray for the difficult individuals, asking the Lord to soften our hearts toward them. To love our enemies might be the most difficult part of Jesus's teachings, yet it's one of the primary ways to reflect his heart. If you commit to this practice, you open yourself to being shaped more into his image.

#5 Offer Silent Generosity

Giving in secret strips away that part of us that longs for recognition and admiration. Silent generosity produces the character of Jesus in us in profound ways. In the Gospels, Jesus frequently heals someone, then instructs them not to tell anyone. I wonder if part of the reason he does this is to model what he teaches. (Ironically, everyone knows about many of the secret acts of grace because they are in the gospel stories.) Consider practicing anonymous acts of kindness. Surprise someone with a financial gift. Buy groceries for a family in need. The list goes on. This doesn't mean all our acts of kindness must be covert, but learning to practice this frees us from the need to be seen by others. Remember, God sees what is done in secret and will reward you.

#6 Surrender Anxiety

I'm a pro at feeling anxiety. I carry it in my body far more than I care to admit, but I've grown in establishing boundaries to keep it from overwhelming me. That is not a comprehensive treatment for anxiety, as we often need a variety of practices, relationships, and treatment to help us manage it. As a starting place, here's a simple list of questions you can ask in God's presence (or the presence of a trusted friend):

1. Who makes you most anxious? Why?

2. What situations make you most anxious? Why?

3. In what areas have you been worrying about your life?

4. What's the story your anxiety is feeding you?

5. What kind of space do you need to process your anxiety?

Once you identify the people and situations causing you anxiety, offer them to God. Ask him to guide, protect, and shield you. If you're like me, this needs to be a regular practice.

Jesus's Promise: A Strong Foundation

Jesus makes a bold statement: Those who practice his teachings live on a strong foundation. On the other hand, those who hear his words but do not practice them are overtaken by the storms of life.

When Jesus makes this promise, he's *not* saying that people who practice his teachings will not experience problems. In plenty of other places in the Bible, he reminds us that following him endangers our comfort—and sometimes even our lives. Nonetheless, he promises a level of interior and community stability that makes our lives indestructible. So Jesus ends his masterful manifesto with a great promise: *If you choose the narrow road, your life is secure.*

When we think of security, we likely imagine ease and the lack of disturbance. But security goes far deeper than that. To orient your life around Jesus and his teachings positions you to live with greater attentiveness to God's care and love. What makes us secure is not our circumstances but God's ever-faithful presence in our lives.

And so, dear friend, as we come to the end of our journey, I pray that this particular truth resonates in the deepest part of your being: Jesus's narrow path might not make sense, but it will save your life.

Every day, you and I are being formed and influenced by a myriad of forces. These forces prod us to build our own kingdoms rooted in power, wealth, and a superficial vision of success. I know what it's like to attach my life to the seductive power of this path. But this approach doesn't ulti-mately meet the deepest needs of our souls.

There is a better way. It's not easier—in fact, it leads to a kind of death—but in God's hands, even death can be transformed into newness of life. When you choose to die to hoarding money and choose generosity, something in you is dying, but something else is coming to life. When you choose blessing over cursing someone who is difficult to love, yes, there is a death at work—a death to the part of you formed by rage and unforgiveness—but a new kind of existence springs forth in you. When you opt in for truth-telling and simplicity of speech, the identities you build around deception crumble, and a deeper self, rooted in Christ, begins to surface.

In Jesus and the way of his kingdom, life is available to you. It's a journey to encountering the living God. The ultimate end of the narrow path is not a state of subjective bliss; it's a journey into the very heart of God. A heart that is cross-shaped in nature.

If we desire a life of ever-deepening relationship with God, an existence marked by freedom from interior and cultural idols, a journey that points us to wholeness, peace, and joy, it's not found in the wide path of the world's conventional wisdom. It's found in the narrow path of Jesus.

And that journey can begin today.

ACKNOWLEDGMENTS

This is my third book. I thought writing would get easier. I was wrong. That is why I'm indebted to a number of people who have helped shape this book.

Thanks to my agent, Alex Field. Your steady encouragement has been a gift to me.

I'm incredibly grateful for the team at WaterBrook. Thank you for this partnership. You've made it so enjoyable over the years to be on the team.

This book would not be what it is without the skill and tact of my editor Will Anderson. When I submitted my first full draft, the book needed a lot of work. Thank you for reminding me to "take it to the street" and for your incisive questions and encouragement. I'm grateful to the Lord for connecting us for this project.

Many thanks to my guys, Aaron Stern, Glenn Packiam,

and Shawn Kennedy. Spending time monthly with you has sharpened my thinking and writing. Your friendship is a joy.

Thanks to my Puerto Rican–Australian friend, Arnaldo Santiago. You have read more of my initial drafts than anyone. Your input is always a gift.

I'm profoundly grateful for my children, Karis and Nathan. We talked many times at the dinner table about my book. Thanks for making me feel that you were interested in what I have to say.

To the elders of New Life Fellowship, thank you. I'm so honored and encouraged by the space you give me to write and serve the church around the world.

Unending thanks to my New Life Fellowship sisters and brothers. At the time of this writing, I have been your pastor for over a decade and in the community for more than sixteen years. There's no group of people like you. Thank you for your love, prayers, and affirmation. And thank you for pursuing the narrow path of Jesus.

And finally, to my dear wife, Rosie. My writing journey never would have begun if you hadn't encouraged me to step out in faith. Thank you for your honest feedback, strong encouragement, and tender love.

NOTES

INTRODUCTION
1. Dietrich Bonhoeffer, *The Cost of Discipleship* (New York: Touchstone, 1959), 89.

CHAPTER ONE: UNEXPECTED DISASTER (THE BROAD PATH)
1. G. K. Chesterton, *What's Wrong with the World* (Vancouver: Royal Classics, 2021), 17.

CHAPTER TWO: UNEXPECTED HAPPINESS
1. David Shimer, "Yale's Most Popular Class Ever: Happiness," *The New York Times,* January 26, 2018, www.nytimes.com/2018/01/26/nyregion/at-yale-class-on-happiness-draws-huge-crowd-laurie-santos.html.
2. Ron Rolheiser, "Risking God's Mercy," RonRolheiser.com, October 15, 2000, https://ronrolheiser.com/risking-gods-mercy.
3. Søren Kierkegaard, *Purity of Heart Is to Will One Thing* (New York: Harper, 1948).

CHAPTER THREE: UNEXPECTED RIGHTEOUSNESS
1. Ronald Rolheiser, *Forgotten Among the Lilies: Learning to Live Beyond Our Fears* (New York: Image, 2007), 13.

2. Eugene H. Peterson, *The Pastor: A Memoir* (New York: HarperOne, 2012), 157.

CHAPTER FOUR: OUR WITNESS

1. *The Help*, directed by Tate Taylor (Beverly Hills: Walt Disney Studios Motion Pictures, 2011).

2. Mark Kurlansky, *Salt: A World History* (New York: Penguin, 2003), 63.

3. Rich Villodas, *The Deeply Formed Life: Five Transformative Values to Root Us in the Way of Jesus* (Colorado Springs: WaterBrook, 2020), 185.

4. Parker Palmer, *Let Your Life Speak: Listening for the Voice of Vocation* (San Francisco: Jossey-Bass, 2000), 78.

CHAPTER FIVE: OUR ANGER

1. Barbara Holmes, quoted in "Contemplating Anger," Center for Action and Contemplation, June 9, 2020, https://cac.org/daily-meditations/contemplating-anger-2020-06-09.

2. Dale Bruner, *Matthew: A Commentary, Volume 1* (Grand Rapids: Eerdmans, 2007), 208.

3. Dallas Willard, *Divine Conspiracy: Rediscovering Our Hidden Life in God* (New York: HarperSanFrancisco, 1998), 150.

4. Bruner (quoting an English proverb), *Matthew*, 209.

5. Bill Hathaway, " 'Likes' and 'Shares' Teach People to Express More Outrage Online," YaleNews, August 13, 2021, https://news.yale.edu/2021/08/13/likes-and-shares-teach-people-express-more-outrage-online.

CHAPTER SIX: OUR WORDS

1. Stanley Hauerwas, "How Do I Get Through the Day Without Telling a Lie?," The Examined Life, January 2017, https://examined-life.com/interviews/stanley-hauwerwas.

2. Ron Rolheiser, "Playing Loose with the Truth," Oblate School of Theology, December 1, 2017, https://ost.edu/playing-loose-truth.

3. Dietrich Bonhoeffer, *The Collected Sermons of Dietrich Bonhoeffer*, ed. Isabel Best (Minneapolis: Fortress, 2012), 144.

CHAPTER SEVEN: OUR DESIRES

1. Sr. Miriam James (@onegroovynun), Twitter, May 19, 2018, 5:36 A.M., https://twitter.com/onegroovynun/status/997803197459845120.

2. Alexis Kleinman, "Porn Sites Get More Visitors Each Month Than Netflix, Amazon and Twitter Combined," HuffPost, December 6, 2017, www.huffpost.com/entry/internet-porn-stats_n_3187682.

3. "Internet Pornography by the Numbers; A Significant Threat to So-

ciety," Webroot, www.webroot.com/us/en/resources/tips-articles/internet-pornography-by-the-numbers.

4. "Internet Pornography."

5. Kleinman, "Porn Sites."

6. "Porn in the Digital Age: New Research Reveals 10 Trends," Barna, April 6, 2016, www.barna.com/research/porn-in-the-digital-age-new-research-reveals-10-trends.

7. Sarah Young, "Digisexuals: Number of People Who Prefer Sex with Robots to Surge, Find Experts," *Independent,* November 30, 2017, www.independent.co.uk/life-style/digisexuals-robot-sex-preferences-university-manitoba-canada-identity-a8084096.html.

8. Neil McArthur, quoted in Young, "Digisexuals."

CHAPTER EIGHT: OUR MONEY

1. *HELPS Word-Studies,* s.v., "mammōnás," Bible Hub, https://biblehub.com/greek/3126.htm.

2. Herbert McCabe, *God, Christ and Us,* ed. Brian Davies (New York: Continuum, 2005), 133.

3. John Wesley, *Thirteen Discourses on the Sermon on the Mount* (Franklin, Tenn.: Seedbed, 2014), 190.

4. Leo Tolstoy, *How Much Land Does a Man Need? and Other Stories* (New York: Penguin Classics, 1994), 96.

5. Our worship pastor, Cate Song, and I co-wrote it; "Giving Liturgy," New Life Fellowship Elmhurst, https://elmhurst.newlife.nyc/give.

6. Dale Bruner, *Matthew: A Commentary, Volume 1* (Grand Rapids: Eerdmans, 2007), 321.

7. See Richard Foster, *Celebration of Discipline: The Path to Spiritual Growth* (New York: HarperCollins, 1998), 90.

8. Walter Brueggemann, *Sabbath as Resistance: Saying No to the Culture of Now* (Louisville, Ky.: Westminster John Knox, 2017), 11–12.

9. Richard Foster, *The Challenge of the Disciplined Life: Christian Reflections on Money, Sex, and Power* (New York: HarperOne, 1989), 19.

CHAPTER NINE: OUR ANXIETY

1. Eric Sevareid, *This Is Eric Sevareid* (Berkeley: University of California, 1964), 71–72.

2. Sophie Bethune, "Stress in America 2022: Concerned for the Future, Beset by Inflation," American Psychological Association, October 2022, www.apa.org/news/press/releases/stress/2022/concerned-future-inflation.

3. Richard Foster, *Freedom of Simplicity: Finding Harmony in a Complex World* (New York: HarperOne, 2005), 13.

4. Brennan Manning, *The Relentless Tenderness of Jesus* (Grand Rapids: Revell, 2005), 17–18.

5. *Henri Nouwen: Writings Selected with an Introduction by Robert Jonas,* ed. Robert Ellsberg (Maryknoll, New York: Orbis, 1998), 55.

CHAPTER TEN: OUR JUDGMENTS

1. Gregory Boyd, *Repenting of Religion: Turning from Judgment to the Love of God* (Grand Rapids: Baker, 2004), 13–14.

2. "What Millennials Want When They Visit Church," Barna, March 4, 2015, www.barna.com/research/what-millennials-want-when-they-visit-church.

3. Jim Wallis, "Bernie Sanders Got Christian Theology Wrong. But He's Right About Islamophobia," *The Washington Post,* June 12, 2017, www.washingtonpost.com/posteverything/wp/2017/06/12/bernie-sanders-got-christian-theology-wrong-but-hes-right-about-islamophobia.

4. Howard Thurman, *Meditations of the Heart* (Boston: Beacon, 1999), 40.

5. Abba Joseph, quoted in Rowan Williams, *Where God Happens: Discovering Christ in One Another* (Boston: New Seeds, 2007), 17.

6. Peter Scazzero and Geri Scazzero, *Emotionally Healthy Relationships Workbook: Discipleship That Deeply Changes Your Relationship with Others* (Grand Rapids: Zondervan, 2017), 28.

CHAPTER ELEVEN: OUR DECISIONS

1. Martin Luther King, Jr., "I've Been to the Mountaintop" (speech, Bishop Charles Mason Temple, Memphis, Tennessee, April 3, 1968); see also "Here Is the Speech Martin Luther King Jr. Gave the Night Before He Died," CNN, April 4, 2018, www.cnn.com/2018/04/04/us/martin-luther-king-jr-mountaintop-speech-trnd/index.html.

2. C. S. Lewis, *Reflections on the Psalms* (Grand Rapids: HarperOne, 2017), 36, emphasis added.

3. Adam Neder, *Theology as a Way of Life: On Teaching and Learning the Christian Faith* (Grand Rapids: Baker Academic, 2019), 76.

4. Justin Whitmel Earley, "A Bedtime Blessing of Gospel Love," *Habits of the Household: Practicing the Story of God in Everyday Family Rhythms* (Grand Rapids: Zondervan, 2021), 205.

CHAPTER TWELVE: OUR ENEMIES

1. Tom Weston, quoted in Anne Lamott, *Bird by Bird: Some Instructions on Writing and Life* (New York: Anchor, 1995), 21.

2. Benedictine monk William Meninger once visited our church and shared this prayer in a handout.

3. Dietrich Bonhoeffer, *The Collected Sermons of Dietrich Bonhoeffer,* ed. Isabel Best (Minneapolis: Fortress, 2012), 144.

4. James Baldwin, *Nobody Knows My Name: More Notes of a Native Son* (New York: Vintage, 1993), 71.

ABOUT THE AUTHOR

RICH VILLODAS is the author of *The Deeply Formed Life* (a 2021 *Christianity Today* Book Award winner) and *Good and Beautiful and Kind* as well as a key speaker around the world on matters of spiritual formation. Since 2013, he's been the lead pastor of New Life Fellowship, a large multiracial church with more than seventy-five countries represented, in Elmhurst, Queens, and Long Island, New York. Rich graduated with a bachelor of arts in pastoral ministry and theology from Nyack College. He went on to complete his master of divinity from Alliance Theological Seminary. He's been married to Rosie since 2006, and they have two beautiful children, Karis and Nathan.

ABOUT THE TYPE

This book was set in Galliard, a typeface designed in 1978 by Matthew Carter (b. 1937) for the Mergenthaler Linotype Company. Galliard is based on the sixteenth-century typefaces of Robert Granjon (1513–89).

Discover Five Transformative Values to Root Us in the Way of Jesus

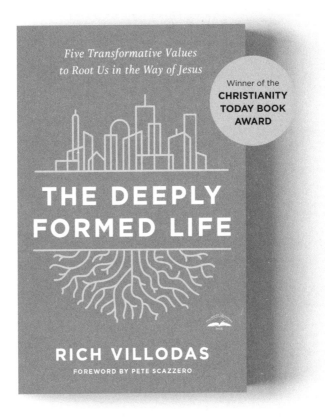

"*The Deeply Formed Life* is a book for our time.
This is spiritual formation for the future of the church."
—John Mark Comer

 **WATERBROOK**

RichVillodas.com

Also from Bestselling Author
RICH VILLODAS

Filled with fresh energy, classic truth, and practical solutions, this is your road map for stepping beyond distraction and division to love like Jesus.

"A stunning book with power to reshape our world…if we let it."
—**Glenn Packiam,** pastor and author of *Blessed Broken Given*

RichVillodas.com